The Naked Mole-Rat Mystery

Scientific Sleuths at Work

by Gail Jarrow and Paul Sherman

 Lerner Publications Company ■ Minneapolis, Minnesota

For Robert
   —G.J.

For Cindy, Philip, Laura, and Peter Sherman
                              —P.S.

Photo Credits

Raymond A. Mendez: 1, 5, 7, 40, 45, 51, 52, 55, 63, 66, 68, 71, 77, 79, 98
Jennifer U. M. Jarvis: 13, 19, 20, 35, 58, 87, 88
Paul W. Sherman: 32

Jarrow, Gail.
   The naked mole-rat mystery : scientific sleuths at work / by Gail
Jarrow & Paul Sherman.
      p.   cm.
   Includes index.
   ISBN 0–8225–2853–3 (alk. paper)
   1. Naked mole-rat—Juvenile literature. [1. Naked mole rat.
2. Rodents.] I. Sherman, Paul W., 1949–   . II. Title.
QL737.R628J37   1996
599.32'34—dc20   95–13381

Manufactured in the United States of America
1 2 3 4 5 6 – JR – 01 00 99 98 97 96

Contents

Chapter One

Picture This...

Picture an animal that looks like a hot dog left in the micro-wave too long. Add four large buckteeth and a long, skinny tail. Imagine that this animal is hairless except for a few whiskers on its cheeks and lips, scattered hairs on its body and tail, and tiny fringes of hair between its toes.

Now, visualize this wrinkly skinned creature living its entire life underground. It eats roots, bulbs, and tubers, and digs a complicated maze of tunnels using its protruding front teeth.

Imagine that the animal lives in a group composed of a queen and her servants, much like an ant colony. The queen gives birth to all the babies and provides them with milk. The servants—which do not reproduce—dig tunnels, find food, and fight enemies.

And finally, imagine that, like reptiles and amphibians, this animal's body temperature changes with the temperature of its surroundings.

This is what you end up with: an animal that gives birth and nurses its young like a *mammal,* keeps warm like a *reptile,* and lives in colonies like a social *insect.* Sounds like a strange crea-ture from a science fiction movie, doesn't it? Believe it or not, this animal is real. It's the naked mole-rat of eastern Africa.

Biologists are fascinated by the naked mole-rat because it's unique among mammals in the way it looks and acts, in the way

For over 150 years, biologists have been searching for clues as to why the naked mole-rat has developed so many unusual characteristics.

its body works, and in the way it lives.

The naked mole-rat is one of very few vertebrates (animals with backbones) that lives completely underground. It is the only vertebrate that has been found living in colonies of over 100 members, each with a single reproducing female. It is the only known mammal that is almost completely hairless and has a body temperature that changes with its environment.

Why does the naked mole-rat have so many unusual characteristics? This is the mystery that a group of biologists set out to solve. Like detectives, the biologists studied the mole-rats and searched for clues to solve this mystery. Their work was full of exciting discoveries, interesting new ideas, and plenty of surprises. This is their story.

Chapter Two

What Is This Strange Beast?

Discovering the Naked Mole-Rat

The mystery of the naked mole-rat began in 1842. That was the year a German scientist named Ernst Rüppell, on a scientific expedition to collect animals for a museum, visited the East African country of Ethiopia. Rüppell and his colleagues saw small, volcano-shaped mounds of dirt and decided to investigate what was under them. They dug up a gerbil-sized rodent with buckteeth, wrinkled skin, and a few sparse hairs on its cheeks, back, tail, and toes. It looked almost like a miniature walrus.

Based on the animal's anatomy (the shapes and positions of its body parts), Rüppell concluded that the unusual creature was a previously undiscovered species. He published a scientific paper naming the animal *Heterocephalus glaber,* which means "different-headed hairless."

Other scientists, however, disagreed with Rüppell's claim of finding a new animal. They thought that since most rodents are born without hair, he had merely unearthed the baby of some larger furry creature.

But Rüppell didn't give up. His associates collected more of these creatures, both small and much larger ones. Eventually, when they collected reproductively mature individuals, even the critics became convinced that the naked animal was not a baby but a new species of hairless rodent.

Around 1900, scientists from Great Britain and Germany collected animals similar to *Heterocephalus glaber* in Somalia and Kenya, in eastern Africa. Citing differences in size and in the number of molar teeth among their specimens and Rüppell's, these individuals declared in scientific papers that they, too, had found new species of furless rodents.

Today, biologists believe that *all* these animals are members of just one species—the naked mole-rat, *Heterocephalus glaber*, which is part of the African rodent family Bathyergidae. The differences observed among naked mole-rat specimens are like the normal variations found within most species, such as the differences in height and tooth structure among humans.

The family Bathyergidae evolved in Africa about 26 million years ago during the Miocene epoch. This was a period when many modern mammals, including the dog, first appeared. Fossils that look like skeletons of modern naked mole-rats have been found in rocks that are 3 million years old.

The skeleton of a naked mole-rat

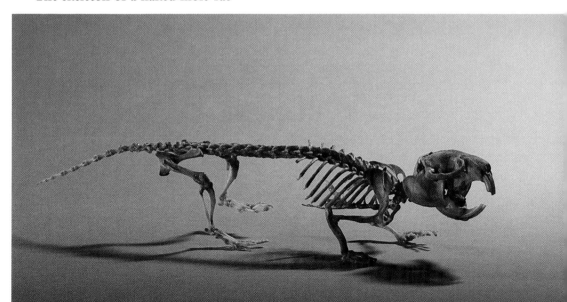

Scientific Classification

The system of classification used today was introduced in the 1750s by Carolus Linnaeus. An organism's classification defines its relationship to other living things, from the most distant relationship (kingdom) to the closest relationship (species). The order of classification proceeds from kingdom to phylum, class, order, family, genus, and species. The science of classifying organisms is called systematics.

Scientists determine how closely organisms are related to one another by studying their physical characteristics, including their shape, form, and structure. The life cycle of an organism is further evidence of its relationship to other groups. For example, mammals produce young by live birth. This differs from other vertebrates such as birds and amphibians, which usually produce young by laying eggs. Additional information about an organism's family tree is often found in its geographic distribution and in the fossil record. Recently, scientists have also begun studying DNA (deoxyribonucleic acid) to learn about the relationships among organisms. The genetic makeup (DNA sequence) of two groups that are closely related is more similar than that of two groups that are distantly related.

Naked mole-rats belong to the animal kingdom. Their phylum is Chordata, which includes all animals with a spinal cord. A subphylum of Chordata is Vertebrata, the animals that also possess a segmented backbone around the spinal cord. Vertebrates include the classes of fish, amphibians, reptiles, birds, and mammals. Naked mole-rats belong to the class Mammalia, which includes vertebrates that have body hair at some period in their lives, and whose young are born alive and nourished on milk from the mother's mammary glands. Naked mole-rats are grouped in the order Rodentia (along with mice, rats, squirrels, gophers, porcupines, beavers), the family Bathyergidae, the genus *Heterocephalus,* and finally the species *glaber.*

The naked mole-rat is classified as a mammal because of its body structure and life cycle. But it is unlike most other mammals because it has very little body hair and because it is not able to maintain a constant body temperature when the temperature in its environment changes more than a few degrees. Furthermore, the naked mole-rat's highly social lifestyle and underground existence are unusual for mammals.

Each living creature is given a unique name based on its genus and species. The naked mole-rat's scientific name is *Heterocephalus glaber,* which means "different-headed hairless." Two organisms are classified as the same species if they can interbreed and produce fertile offspring, young which can also reproduce. Members of a species resemble each other physically, so scientists look for such similarities and differences in body form and function when they consider if an organism is truly a new species. If the specimens are not alive, it is not possible to know whether the organism can interbreed with another known species. Then, the physical characteristics and the geographic range of the two organisms become the only clues.

The differences in anatomy among specimens of naked mole-rats, such as number of molar teeth and body size, created the disagreement between Rüppell and other scientists. Each researcher who examined different individual naked mole-rats formed an opinion about whether the rodent represented a new species. By writing up these opinions in scientific papers, the scientists shared their ideas with colleagues. The published papers either supported or questioned the findings of other scientists.

Rüppell and his colleagues may have disagreed about the naked mole-rat's species classification because the animals' body sizes vary greatly depending on ecological and social conditions. It's likely that the collections made by early scientists were from diverse areas of eastern Africa, containing different amounts and kinds of food. In addition, the captured animals were probably of various ages and social status. The physical differences in these specimens led scientists to different conclusions about the naked mole-rat's species classification. To clear up the confusion, scientists are using new genetic techniques to study the animal's DNA, which is not affected by the environment of the individual animal.

Today, scientists recognize 12 species (5 genera) of bathyergid mole-rats. The naked mole-rat shares certain important characteristics with the other species in its family: its chisel-like, protruding front teeth, or incisors; the shape of its skull and jaw; the area where the jaw muscles attach to the skull; and the number and shape of its cheek teeth, or molars.

When biologists compared the naked mole-rat's skeleton (particularly the skull, jaws, and teeth) to those of other animals, they discovered that the bathyergid mole-rats are neither moles nor rats. Actually, the skeleton and muscles more closely resemble those of guinea pigs, porcupines, and chinchillas. Scientists consider these animals the naked mole-rat's closest living relatives.

Researchers have known about the naked mole-rat's origins and its family tree since the nineteenth century. From 1900 to the 1950s, several biologists dissected specimens caught in Africa to learn about the naked mole-rat's anatomy. In the process of digging into the burrows to catch animals for study, biologists discovered that the naked mole-rat lives in groups within a long burrow system. But since the researchers were primarily interested in the animal's body form, not its social life, they did not investigate further.

The naked mole-rats' habits and lifestyle remained a mystery not only to European scientists but also to people living close to the animals in the East African countries of Ethiopia, Somalia, and Kenya. Naked mole-rats, apparently, are not rare or endangered, but they are well hidden.

Since mole-rats don't leave the safety of their underground burrows, at least not during daylight, few people had ever seen one. Even so, they knew the animals were there. Mole-rats eat farmers' root crops such as sweet potatoes and yams, and they form small volcano-shaped mounds in fields, vacant lots, and

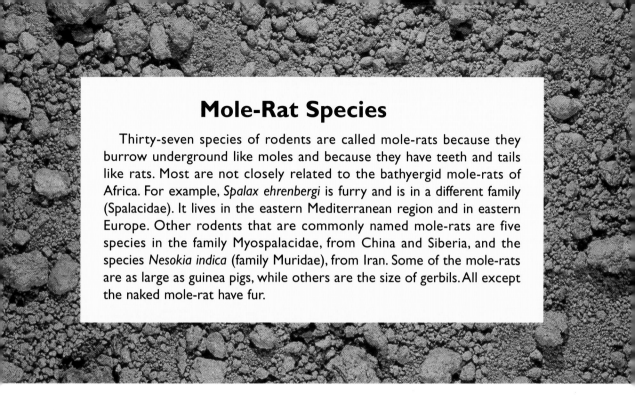

Mole-Rat Species

Thirty-seven species of rodents are called mole-rats because they burrow underground like moles and because they have teeth and tails like rats. Most are not closely related to the bathyergid mole-rats of Africa. For example, *Spalax ehrenbergi* is furry and is in a different family (Spalacidae). It lives in the eastern Mediterranean region and in eastern Europe. Other rodents that are commonly named mole-rats are five species in the family Myospalacidae, from China and Siberia, and the species *Nesokia indica* (family Muridae), from Iran. Some of the mole-rats are as large as guinea pigs, while others are the size of gerbils. All except the naked mole-rat have fur.

dirt roads. Occasionally, observers who were quick and quiet caught a glimpse of a naked mole-rat's hindquarters in a volcano hole as the animal kicked a fine spray of dirt from its burrow.

Except for these rare sightings, naked mole-rats led secret lives below the hard soil of the arid African semideserts. After the initial efforts of classification in the early 1900s, the scientific community mostly ignored the animals. All that changed in the 1970s when a British biologist accidentally made a surprising discovery.

Bringing the Naked Mole-Rat above Ground

While studying zoology at the University of Nairobi, in Kenya, British graduate student Jennifer Jarvis became interested in mammals that lack fur. Jarvis wanted to find out how a poorly insulated mammal regulates its body heat and how it differs from its fur-covered relatives. She chose the bathyergid family because it was found in Kenya, close to her research lab. Since the naked mole-rat was the only hairless mole-rat of all the 12 different bathyergid species, she focused her attention on it.

Jarvis had read the reports published by British collectors in the 1950s. She knew about the animal's anatomy and physiology, about its diet of roots, and about the vocal sounds it sometimes makes. She had read that it lives in groups containing at least 20 individuals. Jarvis also knew that mole-rats do much of their digging right after rain showers when the soil is soft.

Jarvis had to bring the naked mole-rat to the surface so that she could collect information about its physiology—its body temperature, growth rate, and metabolic rate (the speed of chemical and physical processes within the body), for example.

She soon found that this was easier said than done. The naked mole-rat burrows were deep and winding, and the sunbaked soil was as hard as brick. From reading early scientific reports, she knew that ground vibrations chased the mole-rats deep underground, where they were difficult to catch. Jarvis decided to use a clever method of capture described in a 1956 scientific paper.

She dug into one of the shallow burrows, creating an opening. Soon the naked mole-rats came to investigate the damage done to their burrow. When they tried to kick dirt into the hole to close it off, Jarvis blocked the naked mole-rats' return to the main burrow with a shovel. She then grabbed each animal by the tip of its tail and put it in a metal box lined with wood shavings (to absorb urine). She used a metal box because naked mole-rats are able to chew through softer materials such as wood or cardboard.

Because of the difficult digging conditions, Jarvis wasn't able

Newly captured naked mole-rats are kept in a metal box for transport to a researcher's laboratory.

to capture all the animals that lived together in one burrow system. Instead, she collected individuals from several colonies and combined them into one group. She put this group in a glass aquarium in her laboratory at the University of Nairobi. She hoped that the animals would adjust to their new home and companions and would begin to breed.

This, however, did not happen the way Jarvis expected. The mole-rats in the lab colony, especially the females, began to fight viciously. Even animals that had been colony mates in the wild fought each other. After a while, the battles stopped, and one female grew in length and began to breed. This surprised and puzzled Jarvis, since no other mammal was known to increase in length after reaching adulthood. From then on, only that one female in the newly formed colony mated and had pups.

The fighting, it seemed, had not been over space, nor was it due to crowded conditions, since the environment of the aquarium hadn't changed. The animals huddled together after one female began to breed, so they hadn't been fighting for territories either. What had been the reason for the battles?

Jarvis wondered if something was wrong with the other females in the group because they weren't producing babies. Was this the result of living in unfamiliar, confined surroundings with new neighbors?

Another part of the mystery was that in all her months of observing naked mole-rats in the field, Jarvis had never found a pregnant female. She thought perhaps the animals bred only during certain seasons or when conditions were favorable, and she hadn't happened to capture them during those times. But how did this relate to the females in her lab colony? Jarvis put this question aside for further study later.

Although Jarvis was primarily interested in the physiology of the naked mole-rat, as an observant scientist she noticed the animal's behavior, too. When she moved to her permanent position at the University of Cape Town, in South Africa, she took the mole-rats with her. She housed them in Plexiglas tunnels to see what they would do in an arrangement like their burrow system in the wild. She saw that some animals in the colony carried food more frequently than others. By keeping detailed records of their behaviors, she realized that there seemed to be a division of labor within the colony.

Over the next several years, Jarvis captured and brought other groups of naked mole-rats to her lab. She observed that each colony always had only one breeding female. The other colony members divided up the rest of the work in a way that was similar to social insects such as honey bees. Some naked mole-rats acted like housekeepers, moving nesting material and food, and gnawing at dirt that Jarvis added to the tunnels. Others spent time lying around and seemed to do no work at all.

Do the individuals of wild colonies behave in the same way? Jarvis wasn't sure, since no one knew much about the natural life of naked mole-rats. She had many questions, but few answers.

A *Truly Social Mammal?*

Meanwhile, on the other side of the world in the United States, another biologist was studying the evolution of eusocial animals. *Eusocial* means "truly social." Eusocial animals live in family groups made up of parents and offspring. Only a few members of a group produce all the babies. The others work together to care for the young, provide food, and protect the group. This is called cooperative breeding.

To get an idea of what a eusocial society would be like, imagine that your town is ruled by a queen. She is the only one who has children. Everyone else performs special jobs. Some people care for the queen's children. Some provide food for the entire town. Some protect the town from danger. You and everyone in your town are related, but none of you ever has children of your own.

Termites, ants, and some kinds of bees, wasps, aphids, and thrips are examples of animals that live in this way. These eusocial insect colonies contain thousands of individuals, only a few of which reproduce. Most of these species live in the tropics.

Other cooperatively breeding animals also live in family groups in which a few members reproduce and the others help raise the young. Small colonies of bees and wasps live in this way, as do some species of birds and mammals. But unlike the larger colonies of eusocial insects, a helper in these smaller groups may someday become a breeder.

Humans live in social groups with overlapping generations, and children often help raise little brothers and sisters. We are not eusocial, however, because an individual's reproduction is not usually restricted by helping out during childhood. Most humans bear and raise their own children when they become adults.

Biologists once believed that no cooperatively breeding vertebrate was eusocial and that the only eusocial animals were insects. In 1976, Richard Alexander, a biologist who studied animal behavior at the University of Michigan, became interested in why no vertebrates had evolved to be eusocial like the ants and termites. He noted that there are certain traits common to the majority of eusocial species:

- *They nest near to or in the ground, where it's hard for predators to find and attack them. Underground nests can be expanded as a colony grows. As a result of this safe, expansible environment, individuals don't leave their nest, and several generations remain together.*
- *They are likely to be small. As a result, more colony members can fit in a small nest area.*
- *They are likely to live in the tropics where the climate and constant food availability allows for continuous breeding.*

Alexander guessed that a eusocial mammal would have these characteristics, too. Based on these traits, Alexander formed a hypothesis (a guess, or unproved theory) about what a eusocial mammal would be like if it existed.

- *It would be small and live in deep, narrow underground burrows. The burrows would protect this mammal from most predators and could be expanded in length as the colony grew.*
- *It would live in a dry climate in heavy clay soil that would protect the mammal from predators but would be too hard for a single animal to dig through. Therefore, the entire group*

would have to work together to expand the burrows, find food, and fight off predators.

- *Members of a group would work together to obtain enough food for the entire colony with little risk. They probably would eat underground foods such as large roots and tubers and would never need to come to the surface for food.*

One day in 1976, a scientist who was familiar with Jarvis's work in Africa told Alexander about the naked mole-rat. When Alexander learned that this animal had all the characteristics of his hypothetical eusocial mammal, he wrote to Jarvis and explained his hypothesis.

Even though Jarvis had already noticed the division of labor and the single breeding female in her naked mole-rat colonies, Alexander's correspondence pointed out the significance of these unusual behaviors. She took another look at these small, hairless rodents to see if they fit the definition of a eusocial animal. Jarvis realized they were, indeed, real-life eusocial mammals!

No eusocial vertebrate had ever been observed before, but now scientists had discovered that animals other than insects are eusocial. Ironically, it had happened quite by accident: An observant scientist, while caring for the naked mole-rats in her lab, had stumbled on a clue and later, with a colleague's help, understood its importance.

The discovery led to a flood of questions. Why did naked mole-rats evolve to be eusocial? What determines which job each colony member performs? Do male and female mole-rats have different jobs? How does the queen become the only female to breed? How does she rule her colony? Why don't other members of the colony breed? Jarvis, Alexander, and an international team of researchers set out to solve these mysteries.

Chapter Three

What's Going On Underground?

One morning after a rain, a farmer in Kenya went out to check his yams. He was alarmed to see several dirt mounds about 15 cm (6 in.) high near the edge of his field.

He knew that these miniature volcanoes were molehills formed by *uchi fuku,* which are the Swahili words used to refer to naked mole-rats. He also knew that naked mole-rats enjoy eating yams. If he didn't do something fast, the naked mole-rats would dig underground burrows into his field and feast on his tubers.

To stop the thievery, the farmer did some digging himself. He surrounded his field with deep hand-dug trenches that blocked off the mole-rat burrows. His ditches stopped the naked mole-rats from extending their burrows into his yam field and helping themselves to his crops.

Stories like this one made Jarvis and other researchers in the late 1970s curious about what went on in the naked mole-rat burrows, under the hard-packed soil.

No one was sure how extensive the burrows were, how many animals lived together in one colony, or how the animals located food. These were questions that could not be answered by watching mole-rats in a laboratory setting. Biologists had to observe the animals in the wild.

Unfortunately, it's virtually impossible to unearth an entire naked mole-rat burrow system without destroying it. Furthermore, the soil where mole-rats live is extremely hard to dig. But in the early 1980s, Robert Brett, a biologist from the University of London, in Great Britain, came up with ingenious ways to unlock some of the mole-rat's underground secrets.

Gathering Clues

The naked mole-rat volcanoes, about the height of a ballpoint pen, were a sign of trouble to farmers. But to Brett, they were advertising billboards that announced, "Under this volcano is a colony of naked mole-rats at work."

Naked mole-rat volcanoes advertise the whereabouts of underground burrow systems.

Using the volcanoes as clues, Brett located a naked mole-rat colony at his research site in south-central Kenya. His next step in studying the colony was to count the mole-rats. Since the animals don't come above ground, the only way to count them is to catch them.

Brett based his method of capture on the technique used by Jarvis. He dug underneath a freshly formed molehill to find a deeper burrow. Then he scraped away most, but not all, of the soil above the burrow and left one end of the burrow open. Finally, he stuck two thin pieces of straw through the soil into the burrow close to this opening. Brett knew from observations by other researchers, including Jarvis, that the animals are sensitive to certain sounds and vibrations and are easily scared away. So he sat quietly while he waited for the mole-rats to come and repair their burrow.

When the naked mole-rats noticed that their burrow had been damaged, they approached the opening and tried to plug it up with fresh dirt. As a mole-rat passed through the burrow, it touched the straw. The movement of the straw above ground told Brett where the mole-rat was.

A native Kenyan uses a stick to determine the direction of a burrow in preparation for capturing naked mole-rats.

Once he was sure of the animal's location, he pushed a hoe or shovel into the burrow behind the mole-rat. This trapped the animal in the short stretch of open burrow. Being careful not to get bitten by its razor-sharp teeth, Brett grabbed the animal by the tip of its tail and gently lifted it from the burrow.

Brett used this procedure to catch one mole-rat at a time. He placed all the captured mole-rats together in a metal box. He fed them sweet potatoes and kept them out of the hot sun. At the end of the day, he put a piece of sweet potato in the open end of the burrow and covered it with soil.

The next morning, he found tooth marks on the sweet potato, which meant that mole-rats were still inside the burrow. Brett continued to catch animals for four days. He knew he had caught the entire colony when the sweet potato bait had no more tooth marks and there was no evidence that mole-rats had tried to close up the burrow.

Holding the naked mole-rats firmly behind the head or by the tip of the tail, Brett recorded the weight and sex of each animal in the colony. The animals weighed an average of about 31 g (1 oz), and males slightly outnumbered females. Brett marked individuals by declawing different combinations of toes. This way he could tell the animals apart when he recaptured them. After he finished taking notes, he returned the animals to their burrow and used soil to seal off the area where he had trapped them.

Brett could only capture the mole-rats during daylight hours because his study site was too dangerous at night. Lions, leopards, hyenas, and sometimes armed robbers roamed the area when the sun went down.

Despite the difficulties involved in doing research in a dangerous place, after two years Brett had captured 715 individuals from 14 different colonies. He made careful records about the animals he caught.

Based on his observations, Brett confirmed that naked mole-rats, like the eusocial insects, always live in groups. The colonies he studied contained from 25 to more than 295 individuals. In areas where more food (underground plant parts such as bulbs, roots, and tubers) was available, the colonies were larger, separate colonies were located closer together, and individuals weighed more.

Although colony sizes varied, the average number of individuals per colony was 75–80. This proved that naked mole-rats live in social groups that are far larger than those of any other burrowing mammal. These groups are also larger than any other vertebrate that breeds cooperatively.

Brett's research revealed important facts about female mole-rats, too. He succeeded in capturing eight complete colonies and found that each group had only one breeding female who was heavier and longer than most other members of the colony. This proved that the restricted breeding behavior Jarvis had observed in her lab colony also occurs in nature.

Brett discovered litters of mole-rat pups, averaging 10 young per litter. Because he found them at all times of year, he concluded that birth is not related to rainfall, as Jarvis had initially suspected. Jarvis hadn't captured a pregnant female probably because the breeding female is among the last to investigate breaks in the burrow system. Or perhaps the pregnant females are too large to fit into the narrow burrows near the surface, where Jarvis had lured the animals.

Brett's findings provided further proof that naked mole-rats share many characteristics with eusocial insects. They live in colonies in which only a few members breed, and the breeders and helpers differ in body size and shape. The discovery of a *mammal* with these eusocial traits motivated biologists to reinvestigate the social systems of other cooperatively breeding vertebrates.

The Secret Burrow

Brett also studied the layout of the mole-rat colony's burrow system. He knew from studies by Jarvis that a single burrow system could stretch for many meters through the soil. From digging into the soil to capture naked mole-rats, researchers had already learned that burrows lay at different depths.

Brett wanted to find out even more about the naked mole-rat's underground home. Since he couldn't see underneath the surface, he needed some sort of special sensing equipment. He devised a method that worked almost as well as x-ray vision.

Brett started his study by noting where the mole-rat volcanoes were clustered, since he knew that volcanoes marked the location of burrows. This helped him guess where the boundaries of each underground colony might be. Then he selected one colony and hammered wooden pegs into the ground to mark its location. The pegs, placed at intervals 2 m (2.2 yd) apart, formed a grid of squares like a checkerboard in the area surrounding the volcanoes.

Using the pegs as reference points, Brett made a map of the area on graph paper. He would later mark his map with the locations of volcanoes, burrow paths, and food plants. In this way, he could draw a picture of the underground burrow system.

Then Brett captured all the naked mole-rats and put tiny radio transmitter collars on several of them. Equipped with these collars, the mole-rats looked like miniature St. Bernards with rescue kegs under their chins. The transmitters didn't hurt the animals or interfere with their movements.

Brett released the tagged mole-rats back into their burrow. Then he tracked them with a receiver and antenna, the same way people use metal detectors to find coins on a beach. Holding the receiver, he slowly and quietly walked on the ground directly above a moving mole-rat. He knew the tagged mole-rat was scampering about when the beeping radio signal fluctuated in strength. When the signal was louder, Brett could tell he was standing nearly above the tagged animal.

During a day of tracking, Brett noted the position of a tagged mole-rat each hour of the 12 hours of daylight. While he followed an animal's movements, he dropped small flags on the ground to mark the path. Later on, he used the flag locations to plot the positions of the underground burrows on his grid map. He found the nest sites by noting where tagged animals stayed together for long periods of time without moving.

If he stood quietly above the burrow system, Brett sometimes was able to hear underground sounds, such as gnawing on roots and scraping at dirt, made in the shallow burrows. He combined what he heard with what the radio signal told him about the speed at which the tagged animals moved. He then figured out what activity (digging, earth moving, searching for food, eating) was going on in each burrow.

By tracking the animals over a period of 15 months for a total of nearly 2,000 hours, Brett gathered much valuable information about the naked mole-rat's secret life underground. From the map he made with the help of his tagged animals, he described a complete naked mole-rat burrow system.

This colony, which he called Kamboyo-1 because it was near the town of Kamboyo, was home to 87 adult mole-rats. The burrow system sometimes went as deep as 2 m (about 6.5 ft) underground and was made up of more than 3 km (nearly 2 mi) of burrows. This is as long as 33 football fields laid end to end! In fact, Brett thought it might have been even longer since he hadn't tagged every animal in the colony, nor had he taken radio readings every minute. Therefore, he might not have noted some burrows in the system.

The burrow system is like our highway system. It runs to and within areas where roots—the mole-rat's food—grow. The widest road is the main highway. Living quarters (nests) are located on the main highway near food sources. Narrower side streets branch off from the main road. Some side streets lead to food. Some lead to toilets. Some are dead ends. Others lead to volcanoes, where the animals kick out excess dirt that is loosened when they dig new burrows.

The streets closest to the ground surface are superficial burrows. Located within the top 20 cm (8 in.) of soil, these burrows are so narrow that only one mole-rat at a time can pass through them. Most superficial burrows lead to patches of small roots. A few are temporary structures leading to the volcanoes. Sometimes—usually in the morning—the naked mole-rats lie in the most shallow burrows, probably to warm themselves in the sun-heated ground.

Superficial burrows are joined to the main highway of the system by slanted connecting burrows. These lie 20–50 cm (8–20 in.) below the surface and lead deeper underground to the highways.

Like highways for cars and trucks, the highway burrows extend for long distances. But they don't have turns or branches. These smooth-walled burrows are wide enough for two naked mole-rats to pass side by side. Along the way are occasional turn-around spots where mole-rats can back in and change direction. Just as our highways connect homes to shopping centers, the highway burrows connect nests to foraging areas.

Mole-rats build their nests at least 50 cm (about 2 ft) underground on the same level as the highways. The entire colony packs into these football-sized chambers, and the mole-rats snuggle together there while sleeping or resting. The nest, which is lined with grass rootlets and skins of tubers, has several exits. In case of invasion by a predator, the mole-rats can escape out the back doors.

The Kamboyo-1 system studied by Brett had 11 nests widely spaced throughout the more than 3-km (nearly 2-mi) burrow system. By tracking his tagged mole-rats, Brett discovered that occasionally more than one nest was used by the colony. But the animals never used more than two or three nests simultaneously. In fact, the mole-rats used only one section of the exten-

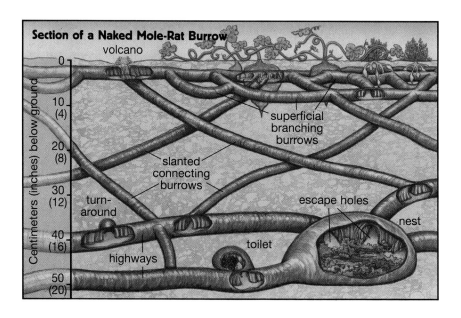

sive burrow system at a time. They stayed in the burrows and nests closest to the best foraging area. When the food in that area ran low, the mole-rats moved to a new area and nest site.

A toilet chamber is located in a dead-end burrow near a nest. Naked mole-rats urinate and defecate only in the toilet chamber. As a result, the rest of the burrow system stays clean. This is important for an animal that lives in groups in such close quarters. If wastes were not kept in one area, disease might spread quickly in a crowded colony.

Brett and other researchers unearthed toilet chambers packed with hard, drying feces but never found evidence of feces mixed with the dirt expelled from the burrows. These findings led them to believe that mole-rats don't clean their toilets. Instead, they apparently abandon a chamber when it becomes full, then dig a new one. This conclusion is supported by observations in the lab, where animals don't remove wastes from the toilet boxes.

Mole-rats maintain their burrows year round. But they dig most of their new burrows during or immediately after the two rainy seasons, October-December and March-May. Brett and others had observed that volcanoing activity is a clear indication of new burrow extensions. From his measurements, Brett found that 70 percent of the volcano dirt kicked up by the colonies he had studied was produced during the few rainy months of a year.

The reason for wet season digging probably has to do with the soil. In the hot dry season, the fine clay soil is baked brick-hard. The rains soften the soil, making it easier for mole-rats to dig and kick dirt out of their burrow. During an extremely heavy rain, however, mole-rats plug the volcano hole with soil to keep water from gushing into the burrow.

Researchers concluded that the mole-rats' main reason for digging is to find food. Interestingly, the animals seem to discover new food by chance. When digging, they don't aim straight for roots. Instead, they appear to dig blindly until they accidentally come upon a plant.

As Brett tracked the mole-rats' burrowing activities, he noticed that animals frequently dug past an area full of roots, apparently unaware that food was so close. They didn't seem to sense food until they bumped into it. Based on this observation, Brett concluded that naked mole-rats probably can't detect food through the soil, possibly because the hard, dry soil doesn't transmit odors well.

This blind search for food takes enormous energy. Mole-rats must gnaw through hard clay soil, sometimes for long distances, before they come across a root. A single animal would likely starve before it found food. But by working as a group, mole-rats can dig more extensive burrows and increase their chances of finding a huge tuber or large patch of roots, enough for the whole colony to share. Biologists think that the advantages of such cooperation may be one reason naked mole-rats live in groups.

Brett's fieldwork described how the naked mole-rat lives in the wild and how its burrow system is laid out. But many questions remained unanswered. Scientists wanted to know more about the mole-rat's behavior, its method of communication, and its social organization. These mysteries were hidden underground in the long, intricate burrows. To find the answers, biologists had to bring more colonies of naked mole-rats "upstairs," where they could see what was going on. So while Brett was studying naked mole-rats in the field, researchers in the United States were studying them in the lab.

Chapter Four

Life in the Plastic Tunnel

Out of Africa

The naked mole-rats' journey in 1979 from the deserts of Kenya to laboratories in the United States took three weeks. The tiny rodents traveled by plane and car. They lived in metal boxes and bathtubs. Their bizarre appearance mystified customs officials.

Their escorts were Richard Alexander, who earlier had suggested the possibility that there might be eusocial mammals, and Paul Sherman, a biologist doing research at the University of California at Berkeley. These scientists had spent the previous month with Jarvis, studying naked mole-rats in their natural surroundings in Kenya.

To learn more about how a mole-rat colony is organized, Sherman and Alexander had planned to take four colonies back to their labs, where they could be observed more closely. The researchers had received permission from the Kenyan and American governments to export the animals to the United States. Sherman was responsible for two groups of naked mole-rats. This is the story of their journey.

One group consisted of 29 mole-rats from one colony plus 2 individuals caught from a different colony. The queens from

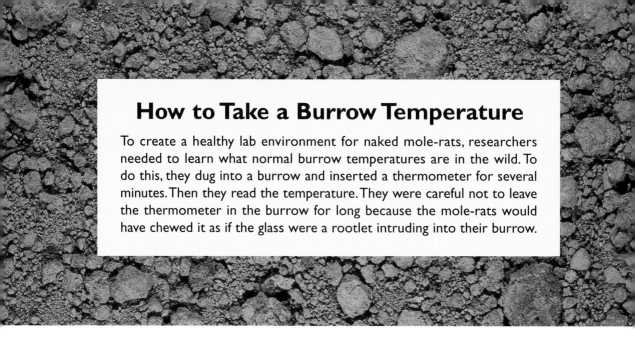

How to Take a Burrow Temperature

To create a healthy lab environment for naked mole-rats, researchers needed to learn what normal burrow temperatures are in the wild. To do this, they dug into a burrow and inserted a thermometer for several minutes. Then they read the temperature. They were careful not to leave the thermometer in the burrow for long because the mole-rats would have chewed it as if the glass were a rootlet intruding into their burrow.

both colonies stayed underground during the trapping, so they weren't captured. Because the researchers weren't able to catch all the members of these two colonies, they combined the animals they had captured into one group. The other group consisted of a single colony of 28 animals, complete with a queen.

Sherman put each group into its own metal box that had been made in Kenya out of flattened gasoline cans. The boxes were about as big as briefcases. He spread grass bedding on the bottoms of the boxes, punched holes in the lids to let in air, and added roots for the mole-rats to eat.

Next came the difficult part. Sherman knew from Jarvis's temperature readings in Kenya that the mole-rats were accustomed to burrow temperatures of 28°–32°C (82°–89°F). The baggage compartment of the airplane, where animals usually travel, was much colder. The mole-rats would have been chilled and even might have died under those conditions.

To solve this problem, Sherman carried the two metal boxes full of naked mole-rats into the passenger section of the plane.

Throughout the 14-hour flight to the United States, he held the boxes on his lap or placed them at his feet. He used hot water bottles to keep the metal boxes at burrow temperature. About every half hour when the hot water bottles cooled off, Sherman refilled them in the airplane's rest room.

During the final part of the journey to California, a woman sitting next to him asked why she heard scratching noises coming from the metal boxes at his feet. To satisfy her curiosity, he opened one of the lids. The woman peered in at the mass of pink, bucktoothed, hairless creatures. Her mouth dropped open as if she were about to scream in horror. Then she fainted.

Upon arriving in California, Sherman kept the mole-rat colonies in his parents' bathtub, the warmest spot in their house, for a week, until his laboratory at the university was set up.

At Home in the Laboratory

Sherman tried to make the mole-rats' new lab home as similar as possible to their natural habitat because he wanted them to behave as they would in the wild. At the same time, the tunnels—which served as artificial burrows—had to be transparent so that researchers could see what the mole-rats were doing.

He designed separate tunnel systems for his two colonies. Each system was made up of about 20 m (22 yd) of clear Plexiglas tubing. The acrylic plastic was used because it is easy to cut and connect into different configurations. It is also strong enough to withstand frequent gnawing by the mole-rats. Even so, Sherman had to examine the systems regularly for escape holes. He replaced scratched or chewed tunnels every few months.

The Plexiglas tubes, slightly smaller than the diameter of a soda can, fit together to resemble burrows in the wild. The system had straight main tunnels and side tunnels with sharp turns and branches. It contained no air holes or openings. Necessary air seeped in through cracks at the joints.

A naked mole-rat scurries through a tunnel system in Paul Sherman's lab.

Sherman knew from his field observations, as well as those of other researchers, that the naked mole-rat burrow system in nature is quite long. (Several years later, he learned that Brett had mapped a burrow 100 times longer than this lab system.) But Sherman didn't have space in his building for an extensive burrow system. Since mole-rats in nature use only a small portion of their huge burrow at one time, he hoped that the total length would not have a major effect on the animals' behavior.

To provide the mole-rats with nesting and toilet chambers, Sherman used plastic compartments that were about the size of a lunch box. He connected each box to the end of a Plexiglas tube. Soon he noticed that the animals used all the boxes as toilet areas and sometimes even nested in toilets. But Sherman had observed in the wild that mole-rats use only one area as a toilet. Something was wrong.

Then he remembered what he had noticed when excavating colonies in Kenya. While toilet areas were in dead-end chambers close to the nest, nesting chambers had more than one entrance. Sherman rearranged his tunnel system, putting one box at a dead end. He cut additional holes in other boxes and connected tunnels to them so that they had several entrances. This arrangement worked. The mole-rats used the dead-end box as the toilet area and stopped using the nesting boxes as toilets.

Sherman put sand, an effective and readily available material, in the toilet chamber to absorb urine. To the other boxes he added wood shavings and corn husks, which the mole-rats could shred to make soft nests. The mole-rats chose one of the boxes with several entrances as their nesting chamber.

Later, Sherman discovered that the mole-rats preferred to nest in a box that was small enough for the mound of huddling animals to touch the sides and ceiling. Perhaps they felt safer, or even stayed warmer, when huddled close together. By using movable partitions, Sherman could adjust the size of the nest box as the number of animals in the colony changed.

Sherman placed food in one of the nesting boxes or in a tunnel. He wasn't certain exactly what nutrients the mole-rats need to survive. And he knew that the calorie and nutrient content of foods available in the United States are different from that of the foods the animals eat in Kenya. So Sherman chose a wide variety of foods to be sure that the mole-rats received the proper nourishment. He fed them sweet potatoes and yams; corn on the cob; beans and lentils; fruits such as apples, pears, and bananas; and jicama (a round root from Mexico that naked mole-rats love). The animals received no extra water. They got all the water they needed from their food, just as they do in the wild. Sometimes Sherman added commercial dog treats to the tunnel system. This gave the mole-rats a hard food to gnaw on to keep their teeth short and sharp.

The two tunnel systems were set up in a room kept at 28°–32°C (82°–89°F), the temperature of burrows in the wild. Humidity in the room was maintained at 50–65 percent, even though natural burrow humidities were found to be higher (70–90 percent). When the room humidity was adjusted too high, condensation formed in the plastic tubes, resulting in wet nesting material. The somewhat lower humidity kept the air moist enough to prevent the mole-rats' skin from becoming too dry, without producing unhealthy dampness in the tunnels.

To simulate the dark underground environment, the room where Sherman set up the tunnel systems had no overhead lights. Sherman and his students used pen-sized flashlights when they watched the animals. Several lamps with low wattage red bulbs were placed along the tunnels to add some dim light for researchers. Since most rodents can't see red, Sherman thought these bulbs would not affect the mole-rats. But the red lights were a heat source, which the mole-rats used to warm themselves. They behave similarly in the wild when they lie in shallow burrows and soak up surface heat from the ground.

Sherman noticed that human voices, vibrations, and abrupt movements agitated the mole-rats, so the room was soundproofed to shield against sudden sounds and vibrations. To avoid upsetting the animals, Sherman and his students communicated with hand signals or whispered if necessary. To eliminate vibrations, the tunnel systems were placed on boards atop partly inflated rubber inner tubes, which rested on tables with padded feet.

Naked mole-rat colony mates spend much of their time lying in piles in their nest.

To keep track of individual mole-rats, Sherman drew tattoos on the shoulders or back of each member of the two colonies. Male mole-rats were labeled with letters. The largest individuals got A, B, C, etc., and the smallest got X, Y, Z. Females received numbers, with the largest females assigned the lowest numbers. In one colony, the queen was the only animal who was not tattooed; her size—much larger than any other mole-rat—identified her.

Soon the mole-rats made themselves at home. They nibbled at food, often carrying pieces back to colony mates in the nest, the same way wild mole-rats do. The nesting chamber was always filled with a pileup of mole-rats, resting and warming themselves with each other's body heat.

The mole-rats moved through their Plexiglas tunnels like tiny electric trains speeding along a tabletop train track. They scurried forward and scuttled backward. They often traveled with their eyes closed, indicating that they had memorized the layout. If Sherman made a slight change in the tunnel configuration, the animals crashed into the walls the first time, but never again. They seemed to be experts at learning the tunnel maze. But the fact that they crash into new barriers indicates that naked mole-rats do not use an ultrasound navigation system the way bats and dolphins do. These animals, unlike naked mole-rats, make high-frequency sounds that bounce off objects in their path and provide a warning of what's ahead.

Although the mole-rats seemed to thrive in their new home, Sherman knew that his lab tunnel system was different from conditions in nature. There were no deadly predators, no rainstorms to flood the tunnels, and no food shortages. He couldn't duplicate these situations without hurting or killing the mole-rats, which he didn't want to do. He thought, however, that he might be able to supply the mole-rats with one thing they had in nature—soil for digging.

Sherman experimented with a setup like a dirt sandwich that would give the mole-rats plenty of digging soil. He took two large sheets of Plexiglas, about 1 m² (about 1 sq yd), and positioned them the same distance apart as the diameter of a tunnel. Then he put dirt between the Plexiglas sheets. He laid the dirt sandwich flat on a table and released a few mole-rats into the dirt.

The animals dug frantically, making new tunnels and destroying old ones. They rarely rested and did not build a nest. The setup seemed to disrupt normal social organization because the animals appeared always to be trying to escape. In addition, as the soil dried, it caked the animals and the Plexiglas. All that Sherman saw of the mole-rats' activities were dirty shadows. After two weeks, he abandoned the idea of the dirt sandwich and went back to the Plexiglas tubes.

Several labs throughout the world had mole-rat colonies housed in artificial burrows like Sherman's. The researchers all found that even though the laboratory environment differed from the Kenyan dirt burrows in many ways, the naked mole-rats adjusted well. In fact, individual mole-rats in Jarvis's lab in South Africa continue to thrive after more than 20 years. Sherman's and Alexander's mole-rats have lived for over 15 years. This is a phenomenally long time for a gerbil-sized rodent to live, either in the wild or in captivity. Naked mole-rats in the wild seldom live more than 5 years.

D isaster Strikes

After observing his two mole-rat colonies in Berkeley for 10 months, Sherman accepted a new job at Cornell University in Ithaca, New York. This meant he had to move the naked mole-rats. Sherman again took special precautions to keep the mole-rats warm and safe as he flew across the country. Despite his efforts, this trip did not go as smoothly as the trek from Kenya.

For the last part of his journey, Sherman had to travel by car for five hours. He placed the two metal boxes that contained the separate mole-rat colonies directly behind the heater vents in the back of the car. Halfway through his trip, he checked to be sure that the animals were warm enough. He was shocked to find all the members of one colony dead. Apparently carbon monoxide had leaked into the car through the heater, and the naked mole-rats had been asphyxiated. Sherman ended up freezing the animals' bodies to preserve them for later dissection and genetic studies.

Sherman lost not only one of his two mole-rat colonies, but he lost months of research as well. The dead colony had been special because it included the only queen caught in the wild up to that time. Sherman had hoped that this colony would provide unique data about mole-rat social organization. Now he would have to start over with a new colony. Such losses are sad, frustrating, and disheartening to a scientist.

Fortunately, the second colony survived the journey to Cornell University. And the next year, Jarvis helped Sherman by sending him two colonies, both with queens, from her lab in South Africa. The flight attendants kept these animals warm throughout their long plane journey by putting hot water bottles on their metal boxes. With these three colonies, Sherman and his Cornell students were able to continue their investigation into the social behavior and physiology of this unusual mammal.

Chapter Five

A Body for the Burrow

By the mid-1980s, four laboratories in the world had naked mole-rat colonies. The biologists at these laboratories, along with their students, cooperated in continuing to unravel the naked mole-rat mystery. These men and women talked and wrote to each other about their discoveries. They shared ideas. They repeated each other's experiments to see if they got similar results. When they came up with different results, they tried to figure out why. Like detectives, these scientists were searching for clues to solve the naked mole-rat mystery.

The field observations in Kenya provided important clues, supplying information about how the mole-rat behaves in the wild, what it eats, who its predators are, and how its burrows are constructed. The lab observations added more clues, revealing information about the mole-rat's physiology, its reproduction, and its behavior in a colony. Although the mole-rat's life in the lab wasn't the same as in the wild, biologists tried to relate mole-rat behavior in the lab to observations that had been made in the field.

Sometimes the research clues fit together perfectly. But sometimes they didn't, and the biologists realized that key information was missing. Then they needed to do more fieldwork and make more observations in the lab. Finally after several years, a solution to the naked mole-rat mystery began to emerge.

N ot a Pretty Sight

The naked mole-rat may seem ugly, but its body is specially adapted to life underground. It looks unique because it lives in a unique environment.

The deserts of Kenya, Ethiopia, and Somalia are hot and arid, with long, dry seasons and short, intense wet seasons. Animals living above ground must cope with the changing temperatures, rainfall, and humidity. Despite the seasonal fluctuations above ground, the underground mole-rat burrows stay toasty and moist year round. Biologists now believe that it is because of these underground conditions that the naked mole-rat evolved to be quite different from most other mammals, both in appearance and in lifestyle.

Studying the mole-rat's anatomy provided researchers with evidence that its sense of sight is not highly developed. The eyes and the vision centers in the mole-rat's brain are small compared to those of other rodents. From observations in the lab and from studies of the eye lens and retina, researchers believe that the animals can see only fuzzy images, although they can detect light.

Naked mole-rats work in burrows, often with their eyes closed.

The underground world of the naked mole-rat is always dark. This could be why naked mole-rats, like cave-dwelling creatures, have poor eyesight. These animals have little need for vision. In fact, naked mole-rats usually travel in the lab tunnels with their eyes closed, which probably protects their eyes from dirt and dust. Scientists hypothesize that the mole-rat's vision gradually deteriorated over many, many generations.

More evidence of poor vision comes from further observations of naked mole-rats. When researchers placed them on a tabletop, the animals walked right off the edge. The surprised researchers, who had not expected the mole-rats to fall over the side, had to catch them before they hit the floor! The mole-rats probably couldn't see the table's edges well because they're used to living underground. In burrows, mole-rats are not likely to encounter areas where the ground underfoot suddenly drops away; therefore, they have not evolved to recognize edges.

Another physical difference between naked mole-rats and most mammals is that the naked mole-rat is almost hairless. But unlike other nearly hairless mammals such as humans, whales, and elephants, the mole-rat is poikilothermic instead of homeothermic.

Homeothermic, nearly hairless mammals maintain a constant body temperature despite changes in the temperature of their surroundings. Special adaptations help them do this. We humans have sweat glands to help cool our bodies, and a fat layer under our skin to keep in body heat. The first humans lived in tropical climates, where air temperatures stay comfortably warm. We have been able to survive in cold climates because we invented clothing and shelter and learned how to use fire.

Another group of nearly hairless homeothermic mammals, whales and dolphins, have thick insulating layers of fat that keep in heat. Armored mammals (armadillos) have a fat layer under their protective bony shells. Elephants, hippopotamuses, and rhinoceroses have thick, leathery skin, as well as layers of fat.

Regulating Body Temperature

Many people refer to animals as being warm- or cold-blooded. Biologists, however, use other terms that more accurately describe the way an animal regulates its body temperature.

The words *homeothermic* and *poikilothermic* refer to the amount of fluctuation in an animal's body temperature. A homeotherm's temperature remains relatively constant, while a poikilotherm's body temperature changes.

The terms *ectothermic* and *endothermic* refer to an animal's heat source. An ectotherm obtains most of its body heat from its external environment such as the sun or the ground. Ectotherms are not well insulated, so they cannot retain the internal heat produced by their metabolism. Therefore, their body temperature is determined by the amount of heat in their environment.

An endotherm's metabolism, rather than its environment, determines its body temperature. Endotherms create their own internal heat, most of which is retained because they have insulation such as fur or fat. The only animals that are always endothermic are birds and mammals. Other types of animals, such as honey bees, may be endothermic when engaged in certain activities during which their metabolism creates higher levels of heat than normal. But this is a temporary condition.

Poikilothermic animals are usually ectothermic as well. Reptiles, fish, and amphibians are considered both ectothermic and poikilothermic because they obtain most of their body heat from the environment; as

When biologists studied the anatomy of the naked mole-rat, they found that it was unlike any of these other nearly hairless mammals. By dissecting dead individuals, biologists learned

a result, their body temperature varies depending on the environment.

Many birds and mammals are poikilothermic at certain times. They are not considered ectothermic, however, because they don't obtain their body heat from the environment. Hummingbirds in northern climates are homeothermic during the day; their body temperature remains constant. But at night they go into a dormant state in which their body temperature drops to the air temperature. The hummingbirds save energy because they don't generate much body heat during this time. Hibernating animals such as bears, woodchucks, and ground squirrels are poikilothermic during the winter. Their body temperature drops to just above air temperature, conserving energy at a time when food is not available.

The naked mole-rat is an unusual animal since it can be classified in several of these categories. It is poikilothermic because its body temperature varies with its surroundings. It is ectothermic because it doesn't create enough heat or have enough fat or fur to maintain a constant body temperature. Since the temperature of its natural surroundings remains constant, however, its body temperature stays relatively constant. This makes the naked mole-rat, essentially, homeothermic.

Under special conditions, the naked mole-rat is also endothermic. If a naked mole-rat has a bacterial infection, its body temperature increases endothermically. The temporary rise in temperature probably is due to heat conservation, perhaps from the narrowing of blood vessels near the skin surface, and to increased metabolic activity. The naked mole-rat is unusual because it can be homeothermic, poikilothermic, ectothermic, *and* endothermic.

that the naked mole-rat has thin skin, no sweat glands, and no fat layer. And the naked mole-rat doesn't seem to generate heat by shivering. Most mammals shiver to warm up.

Because the naked mole-rat lacks an insulating layer of fat, it is unable to maintain its temperature by using physiological processes the way other nearly hairless homeothermic mammals do. Measurements on living animals showed that the mole-rat's body temperature varies with the temperature of its surroundings. But since the underground burrows stay a toasty temperature all the time, the naked mole-rat's body temperature also stays constant year round.

Researchers discovered that if the temperature decreased in the lab where mole-rats were kept, the animals huddled more closely together, and individuals were less likely to travel out of the nest into the tunnels. Lab observations have shown that huddling helps individual mole-rats keep warm, but only if the air is no colder than temperatures found in the natural burrow environment. At temperatures colder than these, huddling can't prevent hypothermia, which is below-normal body temperature.

Naked mole-rats have a different way of dealing with hot temperatures. Their skin is wrinkled and extremely thin. In fact, it's so thin that internal organs are visible beneath it. The wrinkles and folds provide increased surface area for heat to leave a mole-rat's body. This helps an overheated mole-rat cool off.

This thin skin and the lack of an insulating layer of fat can also help the naked mole-rat act like a living hot-water bottle. Sherman noticed that sometimes when the temperature in the lab tunnel dropped slightly, certain mole-rats in the colony traveled to the warm areas under the low wattage red lamps used to illuminate the tunnels. These animals basked under a light for a while, then scurried back to the nest and snuggled with colony mates. The heat from their warmed bodies was easily transferred to the other colony members through their thin, uninsulated skin.

Biologists think that because the naked mole-rat lives in a climate that is warm and humid, it doesn't need complex body mechanisms (such as sweat glands for cooling, shivering for heating, and high metabolic rate to turn food into heat energy) to regulate temperature. Neither does the mole-rat need fur to insulate it from cold and heat the way other mammals do. As a result, the naked mole-rat evolved as a hairless, poikilothermic mammal.

It would probably be a disadvantage for the naked mole-rat to be completely covered with fur. Parasites such as lice, mites, and fleas nest in hair, and spread quickly among animals that huddle with companions. Infestations by such parasites could be a constant problem for naked mole-rats if they were fur covered. The naked mole-rat's ability to travel backward in the tunnels might also be limited if it had hair to impede movement.

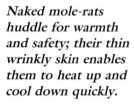

Naked mole-rats huddle for warmth and safety; their thin wrinkly skin enables them to heat up and cool down quickly.

S ensing the Burrow

The few hairs on a mole-rat's body appear to be tactile. When the tips of the hairs are gently touched, the animal moves in response. Researchers examined the naked mole-rat's skin. They discovered concentrations of sensory nerve patches near whiskers and the other occasional hairs on the body and tail, which indicate that these hairs are used for touch.

Lab observations reveal that in their pitch-black tunnels, the nearly blind animals use these hairs much the way people use fingers to feel their way down a dark hallway. As a mole-rat travels forward in a tunnel, its head swishes back and forth, touching the tunnel walls with its whiskers. When it travels backward, its tail, which is half its body length, guides it in the same way. The mole-rat is one of the few mammals that can move backward as fast as it moves forward.

Naked mole-rats appear to be sensitive to vibrations transmitted through the ground or through the plastic tunnel system of a lab. Brett noticed that when he was radio-tracking mole-rats, his movements sometimes disturbed the animals below him. In the lab, vibrations of the tunnels cause sleeping mole-rats to jump up and run around.

Sound travels as vibrations through the air. Because naked mole-rats lack external earlobes, which help other animals direct sound to the ear, biologists wondered about the mole-rat's ability to hear. In the early 1990s, researchers tested how mole-rats respond to various sound frequencies. They found that compared to other mammals, the naked mole-rat has a narrow range of hearing and especially has trouble locating the source of sound. This is not surprising. In a burrow, sounds come only from behind or ahead of an animal, so naked mole-rats have little need for pinpointing sounds from other directions.

Other evidence indicates that the naked mole-rat must use its hearing for communication with colony mates. Researchers in the field and lab have noticed the wide range of vocal sounds produced by the animal, including grunts, chirps, squeaks, squeals, and hisses.

The naked mole-rat's sense of smell seems to be acute. Researchers have observed that when a new visitor enters a laboratory where a tunnel system is housed, the animals become agitated, leaving the nest and scampering about the tunnels. This occurs even if the person stands perfectly still and quiet. But after the person has made many visits and his or her characteristic odor has become familiar, the mole-rats no longer react. Sherman has noticed that the mole-rats in his colonies act uneasy after he begins using a different kind of soap or deodorant.

Although Brett found that the animals could not smell food through the brick-hard Kenyan soil, they may be sensitive to airborne odors, which travel more quickly and easily. Furthermore, the smell of perfume is probably stronger than the chemicals that plant roots produce. Naked mole-rats must have an incredibly well-developed sense of smell to detect and distinguish odors seeping through the joints of a Plexiglas tunnel system.

L iving in the Dark

Naked mole-rats spend their entire lives underground, so researchers wondered if they had a sleep schedule that is synchronized with light and dark (day and night). Sherman and his student Jennifer Davis-Walton designed an experiment to answer this question.

First they wanted to establish the naked mole-rats' usual sleep and wake cycle. Using video cameras to record the mole-rats' behaviors, the researchers watched two lab colonies under normal conditions for five 24-hour periods. Then for 25 days, they turned bright lights on in the lab for 12 hours and turned them off for 12 hours. After the 25 days, they again videotaped the colonies for five 24-hour periods and analyzed the sleep behaviors of individual colony members.

The videotape revealed variations in the amount of time that individual mole-rats slept. The queen slept the least (30-40 percent), the larger individuals slept slightly more, and the smallest slept the most (up to 70 percent of the time). But there was no evidence of a set sleep cycle that corresponded to the light-dark times of the experiment. During the experiment when lights were turned on for half the day, the animals' sleep patterns did not change. The numbers of colony mates asleep and awake at any given time were the same during both the light and dark phases of the experiment.

Sherman and Davis-Walton concluded that naked mole-rats are not sensitive to light-dark phases the way other known mammals are. Mole-rats are neither diurnal (awake during the day) nor nocturnal (awake at night). Individuals sleep at varying times, with no obvious pattern.

Naked mole-rats don't respond to light-dark phases because of their unusual physiology. In dissecting mole-rats that had died, researchers learned that the pineal gland in the brain is smaller in naked mole-rats than in any other known rodent. Scientists believe that this gland controls how some body processes respond to light. In the underground environment, the naked mole-rat doesn't need a special brain sensitivity to light because the amount of light doesn't vary.

Other animals live either a primarily diurnal or nocturnal life to avoid predators or to find food. Or they breed during certain seasons, when temperatures are right and food is more available for the young. Field researchers have discovered that naked mole-rats get all their food underground in a closed environment that is usually protected from predators. Unlike other animals, they not only breed all year round, but they also mate within the colony. They, therefore, do not need to synchronize their reproduction with that of other colonies.

Mole-rats don't appear to be sensitive to seasonal differences in sunlight above ground. The times when they open their burrows to kick out excess dirt are not related to day-night cycles, but rather to soil surface temperature and moisture.

For all these reasons, naked mole-rats do not need the ability to respond to the light cycle. This lack of sleep-wake cycles is probably an advantage for the naked mole-rat. It allows for some workers and defenders to be awake and active at all times.

The Air Down There

Naked mole-rat burrows are sealed except when volcano holes are open for excavation. Since only a little fresh air enters a burrow, oxygen levels are much lower in the burrow than they are in the air above ground. The carbon dioxide levels are much higher. Many animals would suffocate in this environment, but not naked mole-rats.

Researchers wondered how naked mole-rats could survive these stuffy conditions. To find out, they measured the mole-rat's respiration and metabolic rate in the laboratory. They also studied its hemoglobin, a protein that carries oxygen in the blood.

The results of the studies showed that naked mole-rats need little oxygen in their environment to survive. The naked mole-rat's hemoglobin attaches to oxygen molecules more readily than does the hemoglobin of other animals. That helps naked mole-rats pull more oxygen from the air. Furthermore, researchers discovered that the naked mole-rat's metabolic rate is less than half that of other rodents. As a result, it needs less oxygen than most animals its size.

When many individuals live in a closed system that receives little fresh air, disease can be a problem. Although researchers have no data about specific diseases of wild naked mole-rats, it is quite possible that a single sick naked mole-rat could infect an entire colony. But field researchers have observed that the burrow is usually closed off from the surface, and therefore from parasites and airborne diseases. In the lab, sick individuals sit alone in the toilet chamber until they get better or die. As a result, they avoid infecting their colony mates.

Digging a Burrow

The naked mole-rat has a body made for digging tunnels. A mole-rat can roll halfway around inside its loose, wrinkled skin the same way your body moves within loose-fitting clothes. The loose skin and cylindrical body shape help the animal wiggle through the narrow passageways of its burrow system.

Unlike moles and gophers, which dig with their forepaws, mole-rats dig with four razor-sharp front teeth. Hair-fringed lips close behind these incisors and keep soil out of a mole-rat's throat and windpipe while it digs. This adaptation is what gives the mole-rat its odd, bucktoothed appearance.

Brett in the field and Jarvis in the lab first noticed that the animal sharpens its teeth by scraping the top two incisors against the bottom two. The hard soil wears down the teeth, but they grow back within days. Like most rodents, naked mole-rat incisors grow continuously. Jarvis was able to measure the regrowth when some of her laboratory mole-rats broke

Strong wide-spreading jaws and hair-fringed toes help a team of naked mole-rats dig.

front teeth. She observed that teeth grow at a rate of 4-6 mm (about 0.2 in.) a week. This rapid tooth growth is an advantage to an animal that digs with its teeth.

The naked mole-rat's jaw muscles are designed for digging too. The jaw contains 25 percent of the body's muscle mass, the same percentage of muscle mass you have in one leg. In humans, only 1 percent of our muscle mass is located in the jaw.

Biologists were curious about how mole-rats cooperate to dig their burrows. In the wild, it was only possible to see the hind legs of a single mole-rat kicking dirt from an open volcano. To see more, researchers turned to mole-rat colonies in the lab, where they could watch the digging behavior through the clear Plexiglas tunnel system. Small plugs of dirt 15 cm (6 in.) long were added to the tunnels, and the animals' responses were observed. The Plexiglas walls had to be cleaned frequently so that researchers could see the mole-rats clearly. What they saw was a row of busy earth movers.

After observing mole-rats in the lab, researchers figured out how naked mole-rats in the wild probably dig their burrows. Mole-rats line up head to tail. Using its teeth, a digger mole-rat gnaws at dirt at the end of a burrow. When it collects a little pile of loose soil, the digger uses its small forepaws to claw the dirt under its body. Then its hind feet kick the dirt back.

The next mole-rat in line collects the pile of dirt and scuttles backward, using its back feet to sweep the dirt behind it as it moves. The fringe of hair between its toes acts like a broom.

A continuous spray of soil is kicked out of a volcano hole.

The other mole-rats stand on tiptoe and allow the sweeper to pass beneath them.

When the sweeper approaches the surface opening of the burrow, it kicks the dirt to a large individual who is stationed there. This large mole-rat, called the volcanoer, collects the soil and kicks it out of the volcano hole.

The sweeper then returns to the front of the line for more dirt by walking on tiptoe and straddling its sweeping colony mates. The team of sweeper mole-rats forms a conveyor belt system of earth movers that collect soil from the digger and transport it back to the volcanoer. Because the volcanoer is constantly supplied with dirt to eject, the soil spurts out of the volcano hole in a continuous stream. In the wild, this loose dirt forms a miniature volcano above ground.

The mole-rat's body acts like a super power shovel. At one colony in Kenya, Brett measured the amount of dirt kicked out of volcanoes and the average diameter of a burrow. From this he calculated the length of the new burrows dug by the mole-rats. His results indicated that the 87 gerbil-sized members of the Kamboyo-1 colony dug 1 km (0.6 mi) of new burrow in less than three months—with their teeth!

What's for Dinner?

One day while radio-tracking mole-rats, Brett heard chewing directly below his feet. He looked down and saw the shoulder bone of a zebra, probably the leftovers of a lion's meal. Carefully turning over the bone, Brett discovered a mole-rat burrow and tooth marks on the bone.

After examining the tooth marks, he decided that the mole-rats were not simply sharpening their incisors; they were eating. Were they eating the bone to obtain minerals to replace teeth?

How did they know the bone was there? Brett didn't have enough information to answer these questions.

Since insects and worms are found in burrows, researchers wondered whether naked mole-rats might occasionally eat those, too. Jarvis examined the stomach contents of numerous mole-rats from the wild and found no insects. Sherman, however, discovered the hard body parts of termites in mole-rat feces. He also observed that lab mole-rats will eat mealworms when they are offered.

Jarvis and Sherman weren't sure how to explain the differ-

Dissection

Since at least the second century, scientists have studied biology by using dissection, which means cutting apart. A biologist dissecting the body of a plant or animal learns about the organism's anatomy and physiology. This is information that can't be discovered in any other way.

Scientists compare animals to other species by examining the similarities and differences in the internal body structure. For example, early mole-rat researchers dissected dead animals and examined their bones and internal organs to learn how closely related the naked mole-rat is to other rodents.

The dissection and examination of internal organs is also used to learn what diseases afflict an animal and what foods it eats. Examining an animal's stomach contents and feces provides further details about food intake, digestion, and internal parasite infestation. This knowledge, combined with information gathered from observing the behavior of live animals, gives biologists a more complete understanding of their subject.

This naked mole-rat has eaten through its favorite food, a tuber.

ences in their results. Perhaps mole-rats from different areas eat different things. More observations are needed before researchers can form conclusions about these additions to the mole-rat diet.

From observations of food remnants in nest areas and in wild mole-rat feces, researchers know that naked mole-rats eat mainly underground plant parts. Their digestive system contains bacteria, fungi, and special protozoa (microscopic animals). These microorganisms help digest the tough, woody plant material called cellulose. Researchers discovered that the microorganisms in mole-rats' intestines function best at the body temperature of naked mole-rats living in burrows. This is lower than the internal temperature of most mammals. At least some of the bacteria, fungi, and protozoa disappear from the gut after a mole-rat has lived in captivity. How this affects the animal's digestion and other body functions is not known because biologists don't have enough data about wild mole-rats to use as a comparison.

The naked mole-rat's digestive system resembles that of other plant-eating animals. The protozoa in its intestines are similar to those found in the guts of termites and cows. And like rabbits, the mole-rat produces two types of feces. One type is waste. The other type is eaten by the animal itself to replenish the supply of protozoa in the digestive system and to provide added nutrition.

In arid regions, plants survive the long dry seasons by storing sugars and water in enlarged underground roots. These plant storage centers provide both nourishment and water to the mole-rats. The animals munch on the large roots where they find them. They also carry small bulbs and roots back to the nest to share with colony mates.

Some of the roots that mole-rats eat are the size of beach balls, weighing as much as 23 kg (50 lb). When researchers dug up these big roots, they saw an amazing thing. The mole-rats had eaten the fleshy centers, then plugged up the holes with soil, allowing the roots to regenerate. The plants continued to live and grow. The mole-rats returned months later to eat these regrown roots.

Researchers wonder why mole-rats leave part of the root to regrow. Do the plants, when attacked by mole-rats, temporarily produce a foul-tasting chemical that repels the animals? Or is it possible that mole-rats behave like underground farmers, eating only part of a root and cultivating the rest for future growth? The answer is still unclear.

Whatever the reason for the mole-rats' behavior, farming the roots allows a mole-rat colony to survive in a small area without exhausting its food supply. The Kamboyo-l colony that Brett studied in Kenya stayed in the same location over a period of nearly 10 years.

Based on what researchers have observed in the field, a naked mole-rat colony doesn't move. Instead it maintains and expands the same burrow system, periodically moving the nest from one patch of food to another. In the lab, a colony also moves among nest boxes frequently. Sherman noticed this kind of movement when the tunnel, particularly the nest, was disturbed or when food was placed in a different spot. But researchers aren't sure if anything else makes the lab animals move nest sites, so they continue to study this behavior.

Since the mole-rats' food is underground, protected from the heat and drought of the dry season, the animals can gather it during all seasons. The stable food supply is probably one reason naked mole-rats breed all year round, unlike many animals that reproduce only during times when food is plentiful.

The Enemy Approaches

One day during his study of naked mole-rat colonies in Kenya, Brett saw a 4-foot-long (1.2-meter-long) rufous-beaked snake slither up to an active volcano (one from which dirt was being kicked). The poisonous snake glided into the open hole, where a volcanoer was working vigorously. With one swift move, the snake bit the mole-rat.

The rufous-beaked snake, which is poisonous, is one of the naked mole-rat's enemies.

Brett heard alarmed grunts and squeaks from the colony mates in nearby burrows. The mole-rats immediately plugged up the opening to the volcano with dirt, sealing off the snake and the fatally wounded mole-rat from the rest of the burrow system.

On another occasion, a group of researchers watched as a native Kenyan found a snake in a mole-rat burrow. Because so many snakes in Africa are deadly, the man killed the snake first and identified it later. It turned out to be a rufous-beaked snake. One of the biologists cut open the snake's stomach and discovered two dead naked mole-rats.

Observations like these have confirmed that snakes such as the rufous-beaked, sand boa, and mole snakes are the main predators of naked mole-rats. The burrows are too narrow for any other local predator to enter. And no digging predators that live in the area are powerful enough to invade the mole-rats' underground fortresses.

Snakes are most likely to attack when a burrow system is

open and a mole-rat is kicking dirt out the volcano hole. Jarvis discovered that some kinds of snakes are able to smell freshly dug soil and may, therefore, be attracted to a molehill while the mole-rats are at work.

Naked mole-rats avoid snake attacks by doing most of their volcanoing during the early morning hours, when the above-ground air temperatures are cool. Snakes are less active in cool temperatures and less likely to be hunting.

But the mole-rat's strategy isn't perfect. Many mole-rats are still killed or wounded by snake predators, as researchers had observed earlier. Stan Braude, from Washington University in St. Louis, was the first researcher to collect data on such injuries. He studied 28 mole-rat colonies in Kenya from 1986 to 1990. He caught and marked 3,600 individuals, then released them back into their home burrows. Periodically, he recaptured the colonies and examined the animals.

Braude found that many of his recaptured mole-rats had bite marks or had lost parts of toes, tails, and even limbs. He also found dead mole-rats in the stomachs of several snake species. He concluded that mole-rats often fight with snakes, or with each other, and are sometimes injured. In addition, Braude found that nonbreeders live an average of two to three years, and queens live twice as long as the nonbreeders.

In Jarvis's laboratory, mole-rats from one colony accidentally entered a second colony's tunnel and were quickly attacked and pushed back. Part of the reason for such active defense against foreign mole-rats may be to avoid diseases carried by other colonies, as well as to protect the colony's burrow system and food supplies.

Like the search for food, defense against predators and break-ins by foreign mole-rats is most successful when the colony mates work together. Biologists think that this is another reason naked mole-rats live in eusocial groups.

P art of the Mystery Solved

The researchers' field and laboratory work provided valuable clues for solving part of the naked mole-rat mystery. Biologists gathered evidence that helped them understand why naked mole-rats became eusocial. Their hypothesis: the unique environment in which the naked mole-rat lives influenced its evolution as a eusocial animal.

A single mole-rat could not seal off a burrow from a snake invader fast enough to avoid death. Furthermore, a single mole-rat, or even a pair of mole-rats, is unlikely to dig far and fast enough to locate food during the brief rainy periods, when the soil is soft enough to excavate. Working alone, a naked mole-rat would probably die of starvation before reaching food.

Jarvis, Sherman, and Alexander believe that living in a social group helps the naked mole-rat survive in sun-baked soil, where dangerous predators can't be stopped by one mole-rat and where food is widely and irregularly scattered. When it rains, the animals must cooperate and dig rapidly to reach the next food source before the ground again becomes too hard to excavate. When a food patch is found, it is usually large enough to feed the whole colony. Because the underground burrow system can be expanded as the colony grows, mole-rats never have to leave the safety of their fortress to find food or to create new living space.

But scientists still had questions. What jobs do naked mole-rats perform? How do colony mates work together? Additional research in the lab and field helped to solve these mysteries.

Chapter Six

A Job for Everyone

In your town everyone has a special job to do. The community runs smoothly because each person pitches in to get things done. Different people work as police officers, daycare workers, teachers, garbage collectors, carpenters, and road maintenance workers, among other professions. The same sorts of special jobs are done in colonies of eusocial animals.

By observing mole-rat behavior in the wild and within lab colonies, researchers were able to discover how the work in a colony is divided. At the same time that Brett was doing his fieldwork in Kenya, Jarvis and Sherman were observing division of labor in their laboratory colonies in South Africa and in New York.

The researchers learned that most of the time a naked mole-rat lies around, huddling with its colony mates in the nest. But when there is work to be done, each animal goes off to do its job. Every individual in the colony has a job from the time it is two months old. As a mole-rat gets older and larger, its job within the colony may change.

There are three main jobs in a mole-rat colony. The breeders reproduce and care for the offspring. The housekeepers are in charge of maintenance, food gathering, and burrow excavation. The soldiers check out disturbances and fight off invaders such as snake predators or foreign colonies of mole-rats. They also guard the nest. The housekeepers and soldiers include both males and females, but they do not breed.

The Breeders

Only a few individuals in the colony—the queen and her mates—do all the breeding. This system is called reproductive division of labor.

The colony usually has one queen, and she chooses one to three males with whom to mate. They are the male breeders. The job of these males is to mate with the queen and help care for the young pups. Although breeding males may have had another role when they were younger, they rarely do any other job once they begin to reproduce.

The breeders can put all their energy into reproducing because other members of the colony do the rest of the work. Breeders don't have to search for food, build nests, dig new burrows, or defend themselves. The nonbreeding workers perform those tasks. As a result of this "royal treatment," the queen can produce and successfully rear four to five litters a year.

The Housekeepers

While Brett was radio-tracking mole-rats in Kenya, he discovered information about the housekeepers. He noticed that the smaller individuals in a colony are the ones that travel in burrows between food sources and the nest. In addition, he observed that burrow walls are smooth and free of food remnants, rootlets, and debris. The housekeepers keep them remarkably clean.

Brett also noticed that the mole-rats who lie in narrow, shallow burrows directly under sun-heated bare patches of ground are the small mole-rats. These heat gatherers are probably the housekeepers.

This housekeeper is cleaning its burrow walls by biting off rootlets.

To learn more about which animals in a colony are the housekeepers and how they do their jobs, Sherman and his student Eileen Lacey conducted experiments using three lab colonies. Keeping in mind what tasks the animals perform in nature, the researchers put wood shavings (which the mole-rats use for nesting material), food, and loose earth into the Plexiglas tunnel system. Then they recorded which mole-rats cleaned the tunnels, carried food, and swept away the dirt with their feet. They also inserted small wooden dowels through holes drilled in the Plexiglas tunnel walls and noted which mole-rats gnawed them off.

After observing all three colonies for hundreds of hours, Sherman and Lacey concluded that the smaller members of the colony are the housekeepers. Other researchers, including Jarvis, came to the same conclusion.

Sherman and Lacey's results confirmed what Brett had observed in the wild: The housekeepers keep the burrows open and the walls smooth by gnawing off roots. Using their teeth, they lift or drag chunks of dirt and small rocks out of the way. They sweep loose soil to the volcanoer during burrow excavations. (In the lab, housekeepers kick debris into the toilet, since they don't have access to the volcano hole as the wild animals do.) Housekeepers build nests by carrying grasses, rootlets, and skins of bulbs and tubers to the nest chamber. They bring food to the nest for others to eat, and help the breeders care for the young.

In another experiment designed to reveal which animals perform certain tasks, Sherman and Lacey observed digging behavior. They put 20–30 cm (8–12 in.) dirt plugs into lab tunnel systems. Then they recorded which animals gnawed and scratched at the dirt. The two researchers concluded from their observations that the larger nonbreeding mole-rats in the colony did the most digging. This time, however, the clue did not fit perfectly with observations of other biologists.

Soon after Sherman and Lacey reported these results, Jarvis performed digging experiments in her lab tunnels, too. But her experiments indicated that the smaller housekeepers in the colony did the digging.

Jarvis suggested that the difference in results might be due to the way the experiments were set up. She noticed that in tests performed by Sherman and Lacey, dirt plugs were added to the tunnel suddenly. Most of the colony became excited and left the nest to investigate the dirt plugs. As the tunnels became crowded, the smaller animals were pushed aside by larger ones. The bigger mole-rats reached the dirt plugs first, kept the smaller mole-rats behind them, and did the digging.

Jarvis had set up a different experiment in which a pile of

fine sand was put in the tunnel system. As the mole-rats dug at it, more sand was added automatically. Jarvis believed this situation was like the underground conditions in nature.

She observed that when the sand was always present, the mole-rats became less excited about it. Only a few individuals went to investigate and dig at it. Those who did were the smaller members of the colony—the housekeepers. But perhaps they were cleaning the tunnels rather than attempting to excavate new ones.

In his fieldwork in Kenya, Brett found that surface foraging burrows lead to patches of small roots. These burrows are too narrow for the larger mole-rats to enter. He figured, therefore, that they had been dug by the smaller animals of the colony.

As further evidence, when Brett captured an entire colony, he noticed that small mole-rats had more dirt caked between their front teeth than did the larger mole-rats. He concluded that small mole-rats do the digging.

Braude discovered other clues about which mole-rats excavate burrows when he studied several colonies in Kenya. He squirted violet dye on the rear ends of the volcanoers and then captured the whole colony. By weighing all the animals, he learned that the dyed volcanoers were usually the large, heavy colony members.

So, what's the answer? Who does the digging—the small or the large members of the colony? The mystery isn't solved yet, but researchers have some ideas.

Maybe small mole-rats—housekeepers—do most of the digging to find new food and to clear tunnels of loose soil. Large mole-rats, which have bigger teeth and more powerful jaw muscles, are called to action when emergencies like sudden cave-ins occur. Perhaps the volcanoer is a larger mole-rat because its increased strength enables it to kick out excess soil faster and fight off invasions by snakes better. This would be important since the colony is vulnerable when the volcano hole is open. It is also possible that large diggers may sometimes act like soldiers. To test these hypotheses, the researchers must perform more digging experiments and observations in the lab and field.

The Soldiers

When biologists capture mole-rats in the wild, the first ones caught are usually among the largest nonbreeders in the colony. The large individuals are the first to investigate disturbances to the burrow by outsiders such as predators, foreign mole-rats, or curious biologists. These mole-rats are the soldiers.

To observe how naked mole-rats react when their burrow is invaded, Sherman and Lacey set up an experiment in which two separate colonies came face-to-face. This situation could hap-

With jaws opened wide, soldiers from two colonies face off.

pen in nature if one colony were to tunnel into a neighboring burrow system.

They connected the two colonies with a Plexiglas tunnel plugged with dirt. Members of each colony immediately began to dig at the plug, and continued digging until they met.

As soon as the two colonies broke through the dirt plug, the animals faced off. Two mole-rats from each colony positioned themselves side by side and blocked their tunnel. More mole-rats climbed on their backs, making a two-tiered defense wall against the enemy.

The animals stood face-to-face with jaws opened wide, their teeth and noses almost touching. They snapped their incisors and hissed loudly at each other. Sometimes one lashed out and bit an invader's nose.

Sherman and Lacey observed the confrontation for 40 minutes, recording which animals were involved. They performed this experiment a dozen times. No mole-rat ever succeeded in entering the foreign colony because the colonies were separated before any of the animals were injured. But Sherman and Lacey believed that injuries were possible, since an accidental invasion in Jarvis's lab had resulted in injuries and death.

The mole-rats that protected the colony from invasion were the largest nonbreeders. These soldiers scurried to the scene, apparently in response to the hisses and alarm trills of the diggers. Sherman and Lacey observed that the queen sometimes shoved soldiers into the tunnel where the fight was occurring. But she never entered the area herself. Usually the breeding males did not fight either.

How do mole-rats know that intruders are enemies? Odors probably play an important role. Sherman and Lacey observed the soldiers with their noses raised in the air, sniffing as the for-

A naked mole-rat rolls in a toilet chamber to refresh the colony's smell on its body.

eign colony entered the tunnel. The researchers' impressions were that mole-rats are alerted to intruders by smell and perhaps by sound.

Observations of mole-rats in the laboratory reveal that they frequently roll in urine and feces in their toilet chamber. Rolling in urine keeps the smell of the colony on their bodies. This scent may be a form of chemical communication, a way of saying, "I belong to this group." When an intruder gets close enough for mole-rats to smell, the unfamiliar odor probably triggers the colony's vicious defensive behavior.

Sherman and Lacey were also interested in the colony's response to predators. They placed a nonpoisonous milk snake, which couldn't harm the mole-rats, into a Plexiglas tube containing a dirt plug. Then they attached the tube to a mole-rat colony and waited.

As soon as the mole-rats dug through the dirt, they reacted to the snake. First they sniffed at it. Then, opening their jaws and hissing, they backed a short distance away. When the snake moved sideways or tried to slither down the tunnel, one mole-rat nipped it. The researchers quickly removed the snake before it could become seriously injured. The snake had no chance to bite the mole-rats.

In performing this snake experiment many times, Sherman and Lacey noticed that sometimes mole-rats kicked loose sand from the bottom of the tunnel toward the snake. This suggests that the mole-rats were trying to plug the tunnel or to bury the snake before it could attack them, as Brett had observed in the wild.

Unlike the fight with an invading colony, which included many mole-rats, only one or two individuals at a time approached the snake. For 20 minutes (less if the snake was in danger), the researchers recorded which mole-rats threatened the potential predator. Again, the defenders were the larger nonbreeders.

Besides attacking snakes and foreign colonies, the larger non-breeders act like guards. Sherman and Lacey noticed that certain mole-rats, while resting in the nest with all the other members of the colony, lie with their heads and shoulders facing out an opening to a tunnel. These individuals are the first to react to disturbances in distant tunnels. The researchers checked their notes and found that these animals were the same ones that acted as soldiers. By facing outward, the guards are in a better position to protect the queen and her young in the nest.

The Order of Power

In a human family, adults usually have more influence in controlling the home than children do. And among the family's children, the oldest child often bosses around the younger siblings. Researchers were curious about whether certain members of a naked mole-rat colony are dominant over others. How do the soldiers and housekeepers fit into the power hierarchy of the colony? Is one group bossier toward another?

Several years after the division of labor studies were first conducted, Sherman and his student John Schieffelin designed an experiment to answer these questions. They noticed that colony mates sometimes fought over a piece of food, tugging at it and chirping loudly. Eventually, one mole-rat would win the food and go off alone to eat it. They conducted experiments and recorded the winners' identities to learn what characterizes a dominant animal.

Sherman and Schieffelin began their tests 24–28 hours after the colony had last been given food. They placed one cube of yam in the food box nearest the nest. The food cube was small enough that only one animal at a time could eat it. Then they watched what happened to the food, recording the tugging contest winner (the one who ate the food). The winner was considered to be dominant over the animal from whom it wrestled the food.

After observing hundreds of tugging contests in two different colonies, the researchers discovered that the most dominant mole-rats in the colony are the breeders, both male and female. Among nonbreeders, the heaviest mole-rats are dominant over the lighter ones.

Sherman believes that this order of dominance encourages housekeepers to search for food. If food is limited, the larger members of the colony, the breeders and soldiers, claim it first. Occasionally, the housekeepers eat some of the food before bringing it back to the others (if they can do it without being caught by larger colony mates). But it appears that they prefer to eat in the safety of the nest, where food is often taken away from them by the larger animals. Therefore, the housekeepers are forced to continue to search for food until there is enough for them, too.

Changing Jobs

From the beginning of their study of the naked mole-rat lab colonies, Jarvis, Sherman, and their students kept careful records of the animals. Using tattoos to identify individuals in all the labs, the researchers recorded information about each mole-rat, including weight, date of birth, and daily activity within the colony. In analyzing their records, the biologists noticed that the animals did not grow at the same rate. Some gained weight faster than others, and some became soldiers while others remained housekeepers.

The relative sizes of these naked mole-rats hint at their roles in the colony; pup (left), housekeeper (right), and soldier (top).

The researchers found that all mole-rats start off as house-keepers at the age of two months. The animals may stay in this job. Or as their body weight increases, they may become soldiers, who patrol the burrow and guard the nest. They may even become breeders.

In certain colonies, individuals grow at different rates. As a result, some small housekeepers are actually older members of the colony. And some large soldiers, who have grown more quickly, are younger. When colonies start from a pair of breeders, the group needs soldiers immediately. This may explain why soldiers grow rapidly and housekeepers grow more slowly.

In an established colony, growth rates are more similar and jobs are more closely related to age. The small housekeepers are the youngest colony members, and the large soldiers are the oldest. In the well-established Cornell colonies, naked mole-rats change jobs from housekeeping to defense at 35–45 months of age.

Unlike most mammals, naked mole-rats can increase in weight and length even after becoming adults. This happens in two separate situations.

When soldiers are killed by predators, some small adult housekeepers grow faster than others to fill this protective role quickly. Additional lab observations have shown that if some of the housekeepers die, individuals that had been increasing in size stop growing and take on the housekeeping duties. In other cases, if pups are removed from the colony, the smallest housekeepers stay small.

This flexible growth rate maintains the proper balance of housekeepers and soldiers within a colony. Since only a few lab colonies have been studied thoroughly, researchers aren't sure if all naked mole-rat colonies require the same percentage of housekeepers and soldiers.

In the second situation, a few of the adults in a colony (especially females) suddenly grow rapidly when the queen dies. These larger females then battle for breeding rights. The winner becomes the queen. The losers, unless they're killed in this battle for power, remain large and sometimes become soldiers for the colony.

Researchers have concluded from these lab observations that the job activities of nonbreeding naked mole-rats depend on age. They can also be influenced by breeding opportunities and by the colony's need for housekeepers and soldiers.

Scientists don't know how individual mole-rats sense the needs of the colony or what mechanism changes their growth rate, but it's unlikely that the queen's behavior is the stimulus. Researchers do not see the queen performing any special actions toward small colony members when large ones die. In other words, the queen does not appear to tell each mole-rat how fast to grow.

The way in which a mole-rat's role is determined is a mixture of systems found in other eusocial animals. In an ant colony, an individual's size, which stays the same throughout its life, determines its job. In honey bee colonies, all the workers are about the same size but have different jobs, depending on their age. The youngest honey bees tend the queen; the oldest have the most dangerous tasks—foraging outside and protecting the hive. The naked mole-rat's role in the colony can be related to either its age or its size, depending on the situation.

Communication

To coordinate the activities of the colony, mole-rats have a complex system of communication. Individuals keep track of their colony mates by vocalization, feel, and smell.

Biologists have learned that mole-rats have a complicated system of vocal communication. In fact, their constant twittering makes a mole-rat room sound like a cage of cheeping chicks!

After experiments had revealed the different roles of individuals within a colony, Sherman and other researchers tape-recorded vocal sounds of lab colonies. They wrote down what the mole-rats were doing when they made specific sounds.

The researchers identified 18 different types of vocalizations. No other known rodent produces that many sounds, probably because none is as social as the naked mole-rat. Mole-rats hiss when facing an enemy. They trill as a warning of snake predators and grunt before biting. They sneeze when startled and chirp during disagreements with colony mates. Mole-rats also chirp as they move about their tunnels, and the chirping increases in frequency when food is found. These chirps may identify the food finders. The pups have a special call when they beg to be fed. These are only some of the different vocalizations recorded in the lab. If recordings can ever be made under natural conditions in the wild, it is likely that additional vocalizations will be discovered.

Communication through feel is important in the mole-rat colony. Individuals constantly touch each other, using their tactile hairs. They also nuzzle, shove, tug at loose skin, and even nip. These actions might be used to identify each other or to establish dominance. Researchers don't know yet.

Mole-rats use their well-developed sense of smell to identify predators, foreigners, and food. When the queen urinates, she sometimes uses her special call—a soft trill—to bring others to the toilet chamber to rub and roll in her urine. This marks the colony members with her odor. The animals frequently sniff each other and press noses, perhaps to confirm that there are no invaders in the colony.

An experiment performed by Sherman and his student Tim Judd illustrated how the mole-rats use smell to follow a path to food. The researchers placed a door between the nest and a new addition of tunnels in the shape of a rectangle. This addition contained three compartments. In one of the compartments the researchers added small pieces of sweet potato. A single mole-rat was allowed to enter the rectangular tunnel. After finding the food, the animal chirped and carried it to the nest.

Then the researchers put pieces cut from the same sweet potato into all three compartments. They allowed the other mole-rats, one at a time, into the rectangular tunnel. The researchers recorded which path the other mole-rats followed and which compartment they entered. In most cases, the other mole-rats followed the exact path taken by the first mole-rat after it had found the food, and they entered only the compartment chosen by the first mole-rat.

How did the first mole-rat communicate to the others where the food was and how to get it? Did it do a "this way to the food" dance the way honey bees do? The researchers didn't observe any special dance or behavior when the first mole-rat returned to the nest, other than its chirping and waving the food around with its mouth. But the other mole-rats, when released into the rectangular tunnel, usually hesitated and sniffed the air before starting into the tunnel.

Sherman and Judd designed several variations of this experiment to test whether the first mole-rat had communicated by using sound, motion, or odor, which direction to turn in the tunnel system. In one test, the sides of the rectangle were switched after the first mole-rat returned to the nest. If the animal had somehow communicated to its colony mates which way to turn in the tunnel, they would have gone the same way. Instead, however, most of the animals turned in the opposite direction and traveled through the original tunnel.

When the tunnel used by the first mole-rat was replaced with a clean tunnel section, the other mole-rats seemed confused. They eventually went down both sides of the rectangle equally often, which is what one would expect due to chance. Evidently, the first mole-rat left a clue communicating the food's location, and the clue disappeared when the tunnel was replaced.

From these results, the researchers concluded that the first naked mole-rat to locate the food had left a scent trail in the tunnel, which the others followed. The soft chirps made by the first forager probably told the others that it had found food and that the scent trail should be followed.

In the wild, foraging housekeepers don't seem to smell new food sources in the soil. Brett had observed in Kenya that the animals burrow right past nearby food patches and seem to find them only by chance. But once a new food source is discovered or an old one has regrown enough to be used again, the mole-rats probably mark the burrow to this area with a scent for the others in the colony to follow. In a dark tunnel system 3 km (nearly 2 mi) long, exact locations are important.

The researchers had learned which mole-rats do the work in a colony. But more questions remained. How do individuals know when to work and what work to do? What makes them work rather than relax? Which mole-rat is the leader? The answer to all these questions is the same—the queen.

Chapter Seven

Long Live the Queen, Ruler of the Colony!

A queen naked mole-rat roams through a burrow system. Her body, heavier and one-third longer than her colony mates', is intimidating. She approaches a colony member who is sleeping in a tunnel. Putting her face next to his, she opens her mouth.

A worker (left) *freezes in response to shoving by the queen* (right).

Her large incisors nearly touch his head. Suddenly, she hisses and moves forward, shoving the lazy male backward with her nose. After pushing him nearly 1 m (1 yd), she stops.

The small mole-rat curls up, his feet in the air, and lies still. He doesn't stir for several minutes. The queen turns and stalks off. After she leaves, the male scampers to a small cave-in. Sweeping vigorously with his feet, he begins to clear it away. He has received the queen's message loud and clear!

The Bossy Lady

If you watch a naked mole-rat colony for a while, you can tell who is running the show. The queen spends much of her time bossing around her colony mates. She keeps order in the colony and forces lazy mole-rats, like the male with the cave-in, to work.

When a queen rests in a nest, she usually lies on top of the heap of sleeping mole-rats. This is because she comes and goes from the nest frequently as she keeps watch over the colony's needs. She is queen of the mountain!

As she patrols the tunnels, the queen gathers information about food needs and colony activity. When she notices work to be done, she uses her nose to shove others into action. Her shoving behavior increases when the colony is hungry or cold, tunnels are blocked, or a predator enters the burrow. Shoving decreases only when she is about to give birth.

No one dares to resist the queen. The workers usually react to her shoving by moving backward in the tunnel or by freezing as if in terror until she leaves the area. The queen's behavior is effective. Work levels increase dramatically after she makes a tour of the tunnels. Because she keeps workers busy, the colony stays well supplied with food and nesting material, and the tunnels are expanded and defended.

The queen's physical aggression, not her mere presence, gets the colony moving. In experiments where the queen was separated from the rest of the group by a Plexiglas wall full of holes,

The queen usually lies on top of huddling mole-rats in the nest.

work in the lab colony slowed down. When she was removed from the colony, even though shavings soaked with her urine were left behind, workers continued to take it easy. These experiments prove that her smell alone is not enough to keep everyone working.

Without the dominant queen, the colony organization seems to fall apart. In one of the three colonies at Cornell, the queen had reproduced only sporadically since being brought from Kenya, and she had failed to rear a new litter for over seven years. Although she was the largest and most dominant female, she did not appear to exert her power by shoving and tugging at her colony mates as often as the queens in the other lab colonies did. All the mole-rats lay around in the nest. No one worked. The tunnels were filthy. Researchers do not know why she behaved in this way nor why another female did not challenge her for control of the burrow.

The queen bosses some individuals more than others. Sherman and his student Hudson Reeve observed the mole-rat queens of six lab colonies to find out which mole-rats get pushed around the most.

By keeping careful records of the queen's activities, the researchers learned that a queen rarely shoves her siblings or offspring. She is most aggressive toward the larger members of the colony and those who are less closely related to her, regardless of their sex. They may be individuals from a different colony (such as the one at Cornell that is composed of two members caught from different colonies in the wild) or offspring of a different queen during an earlier period.

These individuals are the ones most likely to threaten the queen's position of power. They are also the laziest in the colony—the ones who do the least amount of work when the queen is temporarily removed. Her actions may be designed to keep colony activities going. In addition, by aggressively shoving these lazy individuals, especially the females, a queen guarantees that she is the only one to produce young.

Sometimes a queen uses more extreme methods of prodding. She tugs at the skin of other mole-rats and bites and hisses menacingly. She usually doesn't cause serious injury, though. But if another female suddenly increases in body weight and seems poised to challenge her for power, the queen may attack and try to kill her. The queen usually succeeds.

When a queen singles out an individual by severely shoving or attacking it, the individual sits alone, often in the toilet area. Other colony members join in the bullying, and the mole-rat eventually dies.

Taking Control

Unlike human monarchs, mole-rat queens aren't born rulers. They usually have to fight for power. It can be a long and bloody battle.

When the queen of a colony becomes weak or dies (or is removed by a researcher), many other adult mole-rats, male and female, gain weight. The largest females, regardless of their age, begin to stalk each other in the tunnels. When they meet, they may fight by shoving, biting, or fencing with their incisors.

This struggle for dominance may go on for weeks or months until one female intimidates, cripples, or kills her opponents. Other members of the colony do not join in these fights. But when a loser is seriously wounded, they attack it.

Sometimes males are also killed in these battles for dominance. Researchers were puzzled by the would-be queens' attacks on males because the males might have contributed to the colony's work force once the fight for power had been settled.

The researchers found a possible explanation by observing struggles for power in Cornell's lab. Of the six male mole-rats killed by would-be queens, three were mates of the previous breeding female, and the other three were closely associated (for example, littermates) with rival females. This indicates that male-female pairs may cooperate to gain reproductive dominance. The males may have been killed because their relationships with the female rivals made them a threat to a would-be queen.

After the winner takes control of the colony, her body continues to change. Jarvis x-rayed queens and found that individual vertebrae in their backbones had grown longer as bone material was added to their vertebrae. As a result, the queens' bodies had lengthened. No other known mammal increases in length after reaching adulthood. Scientists don't fully understand how this bone growth occurs.

The queen mole-rat ends up with a body one-third longer than other members of her colony. She is usually heavier, too. The added length allows room for pups to develop in the queen's body without making her so broad that she can't fit through the burrows.

The queen's control over the other members of the colony is powerful. She chooses which male or males will become her mates. The males rarely fight with each other for the right to breed, like males of many other mammal species, apparently because of the queen's control and influence. The queen also stops other females in the colony from reproducing.

Braude and Brett have dug up nearly 50 colonies in the wild. In all but 2, a single queen had total control over breeding. In the other 2 colonies, two females were breeding. The situation lasted for several years, indicating that it was not simply a transition from one queen to another. Why these 2 colonies had two breeding females is unknown.

How does a queen prevent other females from reproducing? Lab experiments helped answer this question. Researchers found that all females in a colony are able to reproduce under the right conditions. But when the queen is around, other females usually do not ovulate or attempt to mate.

When a nonbreeding female was separated from a colony and its queen, she would ovulate and breed even if the researchers put shavings soaked with the queen's urine into her living quarters. This proved that it is not a chemical cue from the queen's body that stops other females from reproducing.

Researchers also observed that the queen bullies the other females in a colony. They measured the females' hormone levels and found evidence of chemical changes in their bodies that prevent ovulation and breeding. Just before the birth of a litter, though, the amount of shoving by a queen decreases. Her body is so bloated and weighted down by the developing pups that she has trouble moving around quickly in the tunnels. Because the queen isn't bullying them as much, the other females experience less stress and become ready to ovulate. If a queen dies while giving birth, which is common, the other females can mate within a week or two.

This situation is unlike ant colonies in which all the workers are permanently sterile. Since all female naked mole-rats have the ability to reproduce, the colony benefits. When a queen dies, reproduction in the colony usually can continue with little interruption, and new workers can be added constantly to the labor force.

Chapter Eight

How the Colony Grows

The queen's role, in addition to managing the colony work force, is to produce pups. It can be a big job. In a single year, one captive queen had five litters totaling 108 pups! Naked mole-rats have litters that are twice as large as those of other small rodents such as mice and gerbils. But the mole-rat queen, unlike the females of other rodent species, has colony mates to help care for herself and her pups.

Mating

The queen chooses one to three males to be her mates. Her choice appears to be related to the males' size rather than their age. The breeders are usually the largest males, at least when they are first chosen. But after several years, breeding males lose weight and develop an emaciated look. They eventually stop eating and die. Nonbreeding males do not deteriorate in this way. Why the breeders do is still a mystery.

All adult males produce sperm, but only chosen breeders mate. If a male breeder dies, other males as young as one year experience an increase in weight. The queen then picks a new mate.

The queen and the breeding males spend much of their time huddling together in the colony's nest. When the queen inspects the tunnel system, at least one of these males typically follows close behind her. None of the nonbreeding mole-rats in the colony follow the queen.

The queen and the breeding males stay well hidden in the burrow and are usually the last to be caught in the wild. Similar observations have been made in the lab. Jarvis reported that on five occasions, two of her Cape Town lab colonies escaped during the night and invaded each other's tunnel system. The next morning, she found several adult mole-rats bitten, but the breeding males and queens were uninjured in the attack.

When a queen is ready to mate, normally two weeks after giving birth, she encourages a male breeder to mount her by making trilling sounds and crouching in front of him. She usually mates numerous times and often with different male breeders. The males rarely fight for her attention. She decides which breeder she will mate with and when. In the lab, naked mole-rats breed all year long. In the wild, too, Brett found pregnant females and newborn pups during all seasons of the year.

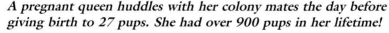

A pregnant queen huddles with her colony mates the day before giving birth to 27 pups. She had over 900 pups in her lifetime!

The gestation period, the length of pregnancy, is 10–11 weeks. In some colonies when the day of birth is near, the nipples of all females *and* males become enlarged, though only the queen is able to produce milk. A chemical cue in the queen's urine may trigger this reaction in her colony mates. Scientists don't know what function the enlargement of nipples serves, since only the queen nurses the young and none of the other colony mates produces milk.

Jarvis, however, noted a relationship between the nipple size of the colony mates before the birth of the litter, and the likelihood that the pups would survive; if the nipples were smaller, the pups were more likely to die.

Researchers haven't established why this relationship exists. One hypothesis is that nipple growth serves as a signal to the queen that other colony members are ready to help care for the litter. Smaller nipples may indicate that they aren't ready. The queen, then, doesn't waste her time and energy nursing pups that would not be properly cared for by the rest of the colony.

Within a day of a litter's birth, the entire colony, which seems aware that pups will soon be born, huddles with the queen in the nest. They continue to gather in the nest for the next three to four weeks while the pups are nursing. This is yet another example of the extraordinary control that the queen has over her subjects.

The Pups

In lab conditions, the queen usually gives birth while moving about in the tunnels. The pups are licked clean and carried to the nest by nonbreeders. After all the pups are born, which can take several hours, the queen returns to the nest to nurse the newborns. She has from 10 to 14 nipples, which is more than

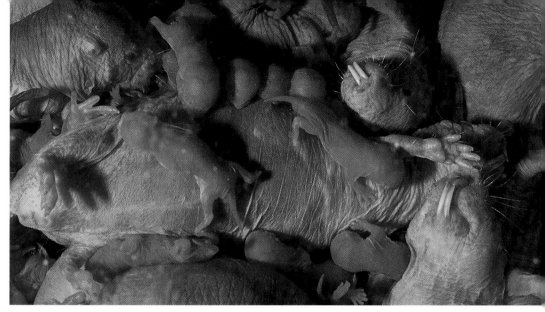

Newborn pups nurse.

the number found in most rodents.

Because researchers haven't been able to observe mole-rats in their underground burrows, they have no information about the birth process in nature. But litters that have been captured in the wild are similar in size to those in the lab—an average of 10 pups in the wild and 12–14 pups in the lab colonies. One exceptionally large lab litter contained 27, while the smallest litter had a single pup.

Like the adults, newborn pups have no fur. They do have cheek whiskers and scattered tactile hairs. Their skin is so thin that their organs and bones are visible. They are able to crawl at birth. Even though they are blind, the pups can sense their mother's presence, probably by smell. The instant she enters the nest, they wobble over to her to nurse.

The breeders are actively involved in pup care. The queen and breeding males lick and groom the young and snuggle close to keep them warm. Younger nonbreeders also help out. Other workers huddle with the pups in the nest, forming a living heated carpet of bodies for the pups to eat, sleep, and crawl on.

Researchers have noticed that the lab colonies seem to be on special alert when newborns are present. At the slightest noise or vibration, the pups are carried from the nest into the tunnels by older animals who grasp them by the neck or belly with their teeth. In the lab, the older animals frantically scurry through the tunnels until the danger has passed.

This behavior may be different from that in the wild because the lab tunnels are so much shorter than burrow systems in nature. It's likely that in the wild, pups are carried to another nest away from the danger site. Researchers have no data from the field to confirm this. But in the lab, if a colony is disturbed severely, the animals will almost always change nest sites.

At the age of two to three weeks, the pups begin to venture into the tunnels and feed themselves. Cecotrophes are their first solid food. These are the soft, green fecal pellets (unlike the regular hard, dry fecal waste) produced by older mole-rats in the colony. The pups beg for the cecotrophes by approach-

A naked mole-rat eats its own cecotrophes.

ing a nonbreeder, giving a call that sounds like a kitten's meow, and nuzzling the adult's anal region.

Cecotrophes may not sound like a tasty treat to you, but they are an important nutrient source for young naked mole-rats. By eating them, the pups ingest microorganisms that will help break down the tough cellulose in their future diet of roots.

Pups spend their time sleeping, wrestling, and fencing with their teeth. Researchers believe that play fighting helps develop motor skills and coordination. It may even determine each pup's eventual social and reproductive status within the litter and the colony.

For the first few weeks, the pups grow slowly. But after one month, they are completely weaned from milk and begin to grow more rapidly. Their eyes open for the first time.

At about two months of age, the young mole-rats start work as housekeepers by foraging for food and carrying it back to the nest for their parents and, eventually, the next litter of pups. Since the queen can mate again within two weeks of giving birth, a new group of brothers and sisters will soon be on the way.

One Big Family

From a biologist's point of view, all living things have one major goal—to pass as many of their genes as possible to the next generation. Why, then, do the nonbreeders in a naked mole-rat colony give up their chances to reproduce, putting up with only a few members of the colony producing the young? The answer goes back to the genes.

Studies of naked mole-rat DNA show that colony mates are almost identical genetically. These individuals are far more closely related than most human brothers and sisters, but not as close as identical twins.

DNA Fingerprints

All living things are made up of tiny structures called cells, which are the sites of most chemical processes within the body. The cell nucleus is the control center that directs these activities.

Just as the cell is the building block of organisms, the atom is the basic unit of chemicals. Two or more atoms bond together into one particle to form a molecule. For example, one atom of carbon and two atoms of oxygen unite to create a carbon dioxide molecule.

DNA, the master molecule of the cell, contains thousands of atoms. The DNA molecule looks like a spiral ladder; scientists call this shape a double helix. The rungs of the ladder contain chemicals called bases. The order of the bases in each DNA molecule creates a special code. The code directs the production of proteins, which in turn control the activity of the cell.

This code is passed on to the next generation through genes, which are sequences of DNA. Genes are arranged in a line on structures called chromosomes, located in the cell nucleus. During sexual reproduction, copies of chromosomes from both parents come together in the fertilized egg. In this way, physical traits (as directed by the DNA)

The mole-rats are genetically similar because the colony is so inbred. The majority (more than 80 percent) of matings are between parent and offspring or between siblings. In addition, queens may have long reigns—at least 10 years in some lab colonies—which means that most members of a colony have the same mother. After many generations, few genetic differ-

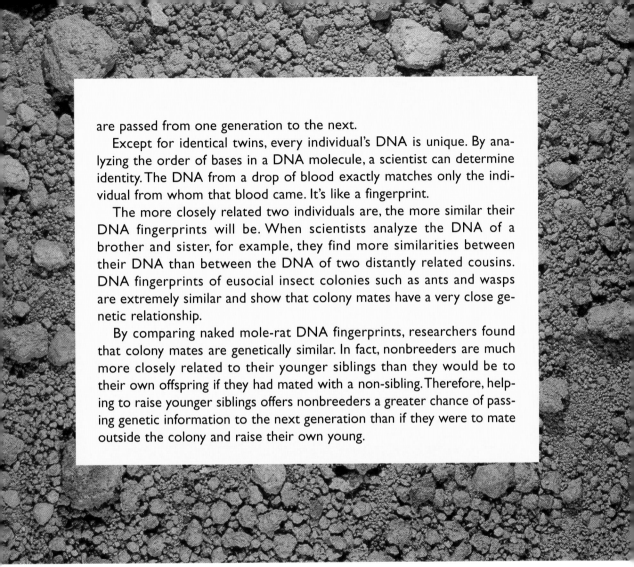

are passed from one generation to the next.

Except for identical twins, every individual's DNA is unique. By analyzing the order of bases in a DNA molecule, a scientist can determine identity. The DNA from a drop of blood exactly matches only the individual from whom that blood came. It's like a fingerprint.

The more closely related two individuals are, the more similar their DNA fingerprints will be. When scientists analyze the DNA of a brother and sister, for example, they find more similarities between their DNA than between the DNA of two distantly related cousins. DNA fingerprints of eusocial insect colonies such as ants and wasps are extremely similar and show that colony mates have a very close genetic relationship.

By comparing naked mole-rat DNA fingerprints, researchers found that colony mates are genetically similar. In fact, nonbreeders are much more closely related to their younger siblings than they would be to their own offspring if they had mated with a non-sibling. Therefore, helping to raise younger siblings offers nonbreeders a greater chance of passing genetic information to the next generation than if they were to mate outside the colony and raise their own young.

ences remain among individuals.

Biologists believe that the mole-rats' close genetic makeup may cause nonbreeders to give up the opportunity to reproduce. They formed this hypothesis after studying mole-rats in nature.

Leaving the colony is risky for a mole-rat. The soil is hard to dig, food is widely scattered, and snakes are a constant threat.

The Eusocial Continuum

Biologists have described eusocial societies as those in which (1) at least two generations live and work together, (2) the group cooperates in taking care of the young, and (3) only a few members reproduce.

While all eusocial societies have a reproductive division of labor, the way jobs are divided among the nonbreeders varies from species to species. In some eusocial societies such as those of paper wasps and dwarf mongooses, all the nonbreeders can do every task. But in larger eusocial societies such as those of ants and termites, groups of nonbreeders have special and different roles.

Some researchers argue that all societies in which a few members reproduce and others cooperate to raise young should be considered eusocial. About 200 species of birds and about 40 species of mammals live in such cooperatively breeding groups. But unlike eusocial insect species such as termites, ants, and social bees, an individual in these vertebrate groups can shift from being a nonbreeder to a breeder over time.

Lions and wild dogs, for example, live in groups of up to two dozen individuals. The group members hunt together and the dominant pair does most of the reproducing. Birds like Florida scrub jays, crows, and California acorn woodpeckers live in groups of fewer than a dozen in which only a few individuals reproduce, and the nonbreeders help feed and protect the chicks. In these groups, nonbreeding helpers will likely have an opportunity to become breeders themselves later in life.

In other species of cooperative breeders, the nonbreeding helpers have a smaller chance of ever becoming breeders themselves. They get the opportunity to reproduce only if a breeder dies or if they leave their home group and go to one that lacks a breeder. Examples include Damaraland mole-rats, wolves, and dwarf mongooses.

Most scientists agree that naked mole-rats should be considered eusocial because of the cooperative care of their young, overlapping generations in a colony, and single breeding female. This combination of factors greatly reduces the chances for an individual ever to become a breeder. But other scientists think that only animals living in large colonies and showing permanent behavioral differences, especially the nonbreeders' physiological inability to reproduce, should be considered "truly social." Furthermore, these scientists believe that other societies with reproductive division of labor are cooperatively breeding societies, but not eusocial.

The new information about the naked mole-rat's social organization, which can be considered both cooperatively breeding and eusocial, has generated excitement and controversy among biologists. This discovery has opened new avenues of research and discussion.

The naked mole-rat has a unique place in the range of animal social systems. Biologists hope that they can gain insight into the social systems of birds, insects, and other mammals by learning more about the naked mole-rat's lifestyle. They want to understand what factors led to the evolution of eusocial and cooperatively breeding behavior in different species all over the world.

Chances are slim that a single mole-rat could survive long enough to find a mate, build a burrow, find food, and reproduce. Staying in the burrow is a safer choice.

If an individual were to leave its colony, it would probably mate with a foreign mole-rat. Then it would pass only half its genetic information to its offspring (the other half would come from its mate, the foreign mole-rat). But instead, the mole-rat stays in its home colony and cares for the pups, who are its nearly identical siblings. This arrangement ensures that almost all the mole-rat's genetic information is passed on to the next generation. In addition, since the queen can produce pups at an astonishing rate, the efforts of a nonbreeder to rear little siblings are particularly worthwhile.

This hypothesis also explains why the younger mole-rats and breeders spend the most time caring for the newborns. Younger mole-rats and breeders are most closely related to the pups. The younger mole-rats, since they were recently born, probably share the same parents. Older mole-rats, however, may be the offspring of breeders that have died.

All in all, the mole-rat's best bet is to stay in the safety of the burrow and help rear its relatives. As pups grow older, they take on jobs that ensure the survival of their colony. By helping to keep the colony thriving—by finding food, building burrows, and fighting predators—nonbreeders are able to pass the greatest number of their genes to the next generation with the least amount of risk to themselves.

Biologists believe naked mole-rats became eusocial for two reasons. One reason has to do with the risks and dangers of a harsh environment that make it difficult for mole-rats to leave their colony and find mates. And the other reason is the genetic advantages of caring for nearly identical siblings.

Chapter Nine

The Detective Work Continues

Piecing together the clues for the naked mole-rat mystery has taken more than 150 years. Researchers now have a clearer picture of how the animals live in their burrows. These scientific sleuths have discovered how a colony is organized and how work is shared. They have observed queens as they gave birth to new colony members and later controlled their behavior.

Biologists also have begun to understand why the naked mole-rat is poikilothermic, hairless, and eusocial. They believe that the animal has evolved its unique physical appearance and eusocial behavior because of its environment.

Since the naked mole-rat lives in burrows with constant warm temperatures, it doesn't need to waste energy on heat-producing mechanisms such as shivering. Its hairlessness enables the mole-rat to act like a hot-water bottle. A mole-rat warms up in the surface tunnels and goes back to the nest, where the heat is transferred to its colony mates by huddling. The lack of fur may also reduce the problem of hair-dwelling parasites such as ticks, lice, and fleas.

The soil is hard and food is widely spread out, so mole-rats have a better chance of surviving if they live in a colony rather than alone. Many individuals working together can dig extensive burrows that lead to food. A group effort is also more effective in fighting off snake predators and other enemies, and in maintaining an underground fortress.

The Unsolved Mysteries

Despite everything researchers have learned about the naked mole-rat, the mystery has not yet been completely solved. In fact, like most scientific mysteries, the solutions may never be discovered. As biologists learn more about the naked mole-rat, they have new questions. Some of those questions can be answered with certainty, but others will stay unsolved mysteries for a long time, maybe forever.

Researchers want to solve as many of these mysteries as they can. To find clues, biologists will use the detective method used by researchers in all branches of science: Make a hypothesis and test it many times to find out if it's true. The mysteries listed below are particularly intriguing.

Mystery #1
How do new colonies form?

After one rainy season in Kenya, Brett discovered two naked mole-rat colonies located quite close together. Between the two colonies, he found evidence of old volcanoes. One colony was large, containing 93 individuals, while the other contained only 25. Both had queens who were reproducing.

Brett hypothesized that large colonies divide to form new ones. He suggested that breakaways occur during the rainy season, when digging is easier. He proposed several possible reasons for splits. The original colony may have become overcrowded. As a result, a small group cut itself off by retreating to a far end of the burrow system and sealing off the burrows. Another possibility is that two queens competed for control, with one of them leaving the original burrow with her offspring. Or a group may have accidentally become separated from the rest of the colony by a cave-in or flash flood that divided the burrow.

To test Brett's hypothesis, researchers must distinguish individual members of several mole-rat colonies with unique marks. Later, the researchers will look for those same animals in small colonies nearby. If any are found, researchers will have evidence that a small colony has split from the main group.

Another way to test Brett's hypothesis is to search for colonies that have been divided in two by a flash flood. Do the mole-rats remain separated, or do they rebuild their burrow under or around the gully that was formed by floodwaters?

One observation in the lab seems to support Brett's hypothesis. Sherman saw a colony divide into two distinct groups after the death of a breeding female. The split occurred along kinship lines, with the closest relatives (younger littermates) going off together into a separate nesting box. The two groups fought each other in tunnels, each apparently guarding the area closest to its own nest. Interestingly, after nearly a year, a new queen emerged from the older group, and the separate groups recombined.

Braude suggested a second hypothesis to explain how new colonies form. His educated guess is that single mole-rats walk across the ground surface at night, meet, mate, and dig a new burrow into the ground, where they establish a new colony.

He bases this hypothesis on observations he made in Kenya several years after Brett's work. While doing field research, Braude discovered five colonies, each containing a single pair of mole-rats and one or two litters of pups. One adult in each colony was already marked, indicating that Braude had captured it previously from a larger colony during his eight-year study in the area. Since the other adult in each pair was unmarked, Braude believed that these animals had come from colonies outside his study site. The evidence indicated that the members of each pair had met and begun a new burrow system.

Braude reported a few rare sightings of naked mole-rats walking on the ground surface during the day. A more probable time for mole-rats to travel on the surface is at night when the temperatures are cooler. Researchers have never been out

Scientists have yet to discover whether naked mole-rats travel above ground to start new colonies.

looking for them at night, however, since it is too dangerous in Kenya to make direct observations after dark.

One way to test the hypothesis that mole-rats travel on the surface at night is to set up low fences around mole-rat colonies, and sink buckets into the ground just inside the fences. If mole-rats leave a colony and head overland at night, the fences will stop them. Forced to turn, the animals will walk along the fences. As they do, they will fall into the buckets. Unable to escape, the mole-rats will be there the next morning when researchers return to the site.

The hypothesis also can be tested by collecting owl pellets in the area around mole-rat burrows. By examining the pellets for bones and teeth, researchers can learn if owls eat naked mole-rats. Since owls can't dig, the only way the nocturnal birds could capture a mole-rat would be if the rodent was scampering across the ground surface at night.

Mystery #2
What does it take to be a queen?

When the queen of a colony dies, only some females increase in size and battle for position as new queen. What factors determine which individuals those will be? Some possibilities are the mole-rats' age, size, growth rate, genetic relationship to the dead queen, or position of dominance in the colony established during pup play.

To discover the answer to this mystery, biologists will observe and take detailed notes on all the individuals in a colony from the time they are born. The notes will include information about all likely factors involved in the females' struggle to be queen.

Whenever a queen dies or is removed from a colony, the researchers will note which females compete for power. By comparing that information to their data on the previous behavior of individuals in the colony, they will be able to form a hypothesis about which factors are important.

The next step will be to test the hypothesis by observing a new colony. If their hypothesis is right, the researchers should be able to predict accurately which females will undergo a growth spurt upon a queen's death. They may even be able to predict which female will be the next queen.

Mystery #3:

Why do mole-rats stop reproducing in captivity?

When biologists first brought the naked mole-rat colonies to their labs, the animals reproduced several times a year. Many young pups were raised successfully. The mole-rats seemed well adjusted to the artificial surroundings of the plastic tunnels.

But after five or six years, some researchers found that their mole-rats were no longer reproducing. Queens occasionally died immediately before giving birth. In other cases, newborns weren't cared for and the queen didn't nurse them. Sometimes the queen continued to mate, but no pups were born.

Jarvis noticed in her colonies that the pups often died within days of birth, even if the queen had plenty of milk to feed them. The newborns were repeatedly moved around the tunnel system by their older siblings. The frequent movement caused injuries and prevented the young from nursing.

Jarvis hypothesized that the lab colonies grew too large, too fast. Without natural predation from snakes, there were too many young mole-rats in the tunnel system, and the balance of the colony was upset. These young animals, by their sheer numbers, interfered with the proper care of the pups.

Jarvis tested her hypothesis during the first few years that she had lab colonies. She set up an experiment to simulate predation by using four of her lab colonies. Two of the colonies were controls; she did nothing to these. The other two were her test colonies. She removed some young mole-rats (who were weaned, but were not yet adults) from each colony. She didn't kill these animals the way a snake would, but removing them from the lab tunnel had the same effect on the colony.

At the end of her two-year experiment, more pups had survived in the colonies where animals had been periodically removed. These results fit her hypothesis, but Jarvis had tested too few colonies to make firm conclusions. Still, the test indicates that removing some animals from a colony might improve pup rearing.

Another hypothesis involves the size of the burrows: Lab tunnels may become too crowded for the colonies since few animals are dying. Because the mole-rats can't expand the tunnels as they would in nature, they stop producing more colony members.

To test this hypothesis, Sherman added more lengths of plastic tunnel to the set-up in his lab. But he found that extending the tunnel made no difference. The mole-rats used only the tunnels closest to their food supply, as they do in nature, and reproduction did not resume.

A different hypothesis is that the mole-rats stop reproducing because they are too old. Perhaps as the breeders age, they produce pups that are less likely to survive. Or maybe the nonbreeders are unable to care for the pups, regardless of how strong and healthy the pups are at birth. Eventually, the breeders stop mating.

Some evidence does fit this hypothesis. Many lab colonies breed successfully for five or six years, which roughly equals a queen mole-rat's life span in the wild. Some of Jarvis's queens, however, are older than this and yet continue to breed successfully. These queens belong to the colonies from which young are removed periodically, indicating that a queen's age may be less important than the number of members in a colony.

Now that zoos have begun housing naked mole-rat colonies, more information about reproduction has come to light. Zoo colonies, unlike those in a lab, have continued to produce young. This may be because conditions in zoos are different from those in labs. The zoo curators frequently subdivide colonies, periodically moving out animals. Sometimes they take out large females who have lost the fight for queenship, and use them to start new colonies. This roughly corresponds to Jarvis's predation experiments.

Another factor involves noise and commotion around the colonies. Because more outside interference occurs at zoos than in laboratories, the zoos' mole-rats experience more disturbances. These disruptions may create a constant need for workers to perform defense and housekeeping duties. Perhaps the animals produce more young to meet this need.

Lab research by Deborah Ciszek at Michigan suggests that removing odors or disturbing the tunnel system may stimulate breeding. As part of an experiment on chemical communication, the mole-rats' toilets were cleaned daily. Soon the queen, who had not produced a litter for several years, began to breed again. Did the disruption to the tunnels or the removal of chemical signals cause this response?

Sherman and Randi Winter designed an experiment to test whether constant disturbances, including predation and the cleaning of tunnels, would stimulate a queen to reproduce and whether a queen's age was also a factor. As a control in the experiment, they used the past years of observations in which the queens (all over six years old) in three test colonies had stopped breeding. During the control period, the three burrow systems had been cleaned occasionally, but disturbances were kept to a minimum.

For the first test colony, they constantly added nesting materials, piles of wood shavings, and barricades of cardboard and cork. Each day they also changed the place in the tunnel system where they added food.

In the second colony, they added shavings, cardboard, and cork to the tunnels and changed the food location daily. But in addition, they disturbed the animals further by catching all the mole-rats in the colony and placing them together in a small box for one-half hour every day.

In the third colony, they did not add material to the tunnels or remove animals. Instead, they cleaned one-third of the tunnels every day.

In less than a month, mating began in the third colony. Breeders in this colony had not mated for four years before this experiment. Mating was not observed, however, in the other colonies used in this experiment. These results indicate that either the lack of smells or the considerable disruption to the tunnel system stimulated mating activity. The results of additional tests hint that rearranging the tunnels in a system is more likely to increase mating behavior than only cleaning the tunnels.

Although insufficient time has passed for Sherman to draw firm conclusions, he hopes that these experiments will provide answers about reproduction. The return of breeding in the third colony gave him a clue to the factors that stimulate a queen to produce more young. Furthermore, it proved that the aging hypothesis is wrong.

Biologists have formed other hypotheses, as well. Perhaps mole-rats raise pups only when the number of workers in the colony drops. Or maybe the animals require special nutrients for reproduction that gradually disappear from their bodies unless replenished by certain foods.

While biologists are curious about the reproduction question, the mystery probably will be solved by zoo curators. They frequently subdivide their colonies, and the naked mole-rats experience regular disturbances from zoo visitors. These may be the very factors that stimulate reproduction.

Mystery #4:
How different are the genes of naked mole-rats in different colonies?

Biologists already know that mole-rats from separate colonies sometimes vary greatly in size. Such size differences are partly due to nutrition. Animals that live in areas where food is plentiful grow larger. But genetic studies indicate that there is more to it than this.

Researchers have found that individuals living in the same naked mole-rat colony have a very similar genetic makeup. Animals from different colonies located in the same small geographic area have more differences in their DNA than those within one colony, but they are still quite similar. This suggests that the separate colonies may have descended from the same mother colony, and that new colonies sometimes form by splitting.

In studies of the DNA of individuals in colonies that are located many kilometers apart, researchers found that the farther apart two colonies are located, the greater the differences in their DNA. In fact, there are as many genetic variations between the groups of naked mole-rats in southern Kenya and northern Kenya, which are only 300 km (190 mi) apart, as there are among the subspecies of some other rodents. Because colonies are isolated in the hard soil, the animals rarely mix and interbreed. Over many thousands of years, naked mole-rats from different areas of eastern Africa may have become as different from each other as the wolves of Alaska are from the coyotes of Arizona.

Are naked mole-rats from distant colonies so different that the animals belong to separate species? Future studies will investigate the DNA of naked mole-rat colonies from all over Kenya, and perhaps Ethiopia and Somalia, to help solve this mystery.

Mystery #5:
Are there other eusocial animals?

Since the discovery of the naked mole-rat's eusociality, biologists have become more interested in why animals develop this lifestyle. What factors make group living an advantage over solitary living? And what factors encourage the development of special characteristics, such as restricted breeding and cooperatively raising young, found in a eusocial society?

One way Jarvis and her student Nigel Bennett have approached this mystery is to study another type of mole-rat closely related to the naked mole-rat but different in important ways.

The Damaraland mole-rat, *Cryptomys damarensis,* is found in the Damaraland region of the Kalahari Desert of southern Africa. It is covered with fur and is homeothermic and endothermic, the way most mammals are. Its colonies are much smaller (averaging 16 individuals) than those of the naked mole-rat. It lives in underground burrow systems, but these burrows are dug in softer soils than the brick-hard earth that forms the naked mole-rat's home. The burrow systems' temperature also varies daily and seasonally.

Biologists now believe that the Damaraland mole-rat is eusocial, too, although not to the same extent as the naked mole-rat. Like the naked mole-rat, only one female and one to three male Damaraland mole-rats breed. But unlike the naked mole-rat, a Damaraland nonbreeder may leave its colony to breed if the original breeder (its parent) has died. A Damaraland mole-rat will not breed with its surviving parent.

The separation from a parent colony occurs when the rains come and glue the powdery sand together like a sand castle at the beach. This enables individuals to dig to another colony. Lab observations have shown that the Damaraland mole-rat is less hostile to mole-rats from another colony than the naked mole-rat is, which means breeding outside the colony is more likely to happen.

These differences among mole-rat species shed light on the environmental factors that lead to eusociality. Some mole-rat species are solitary, rather than social. They live in areas where ample rain allows digging most of the year, and where food is more plentiful and evenly distributed in small patches. The Damaraland and the naked mole-rat, both highly social species, live in drier climates in which digging is possible for only part of the year. The food in these dry climates grows in large patches that are irregularly spaced and widely separated from each other. The important factor in survival is whether a colony is able to extend its burrow to these rich food supplies during the short digging season.

Are differences in food distribution and ease of digging the reasons naked and Damaraland mole-rats are more social than other mole-rat species? Are these also the reasons naked mole-rats are more eusocial than Damaraland mole-rats? Do differences in the type of predators that hunt these animals lead to a variation in social systems?

Researchers can't be sure of the answers to these questions. They think, however, that the unusual features of the naked mole-rat—lack of hair, poikilothermy, huge colonies, and inbreeding—are not necessary for the development of eusociality. After all, the Damaraland mole-rat has none of these features and yet is eusocial, too. More likely, the naked mole-rat evolved these unique characteristics after moving as a group into an underground burrow habitat that is almost completely buffered from temperature and climate changes, and is composed of soil that's impossible to dig for much of the year.

What is the key to whether a subterranean animal develops a eusocial lifestyle? Biologists suspect it is an environment with uneven distribution of food and limited time to locate it. Both factors favor a large group working together to find food and to fight off predators.

Using these two criteria, researchers have gained clues about where other eusocial mammals might be found. They plan to search in dry climates with restricted rainfall and patchy food sources. The researchers will also investigate whether or not predators in these areas are stopped more effectively by a group than by an individual.

Two groups of social, subterranean rodents, the coruros (genus *Spalacopus*) and tuco-tucos (genus *Ctenomys*) of South America, have already been identified for further study. Because these animals live in arid environments and have widely distributed food sources, researchers are interested in comparing their social systems with those of the naked mole-rat. Information gained from this study may give biologists more insight into the factors that favor the development of eusociality.

Calling All Sleuths

As you have been reading this book, naked mole-rat researchers have been continuing their work. They hope to answer the many questions that have emerged from their experiments as well as to solve the existing naked mole-rat mysteries.

Maybe someday you'll be one of those researchers who helps solve the naked mole-rat mysteries. You might be the one who invents an ingenious way to study naked mole-rats underground. Perhaps you'll figure out how to insert a fiber-optic tube into a mole-rat burrow without having the animal mistake it for a root and chew it off. Or you might uncover a new clue about the mole-rat's secret life.

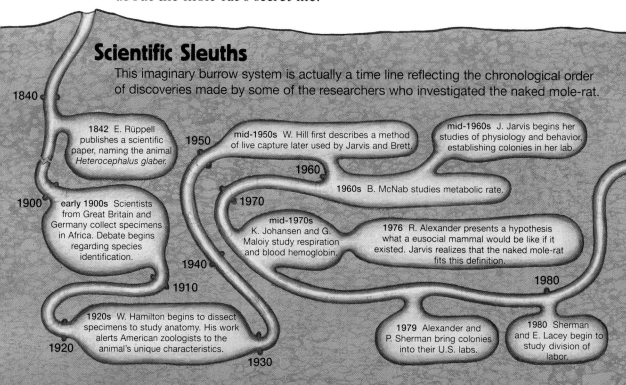

Scientific Sleuths

This imaginary burrow system is actually a time line reflecting the chronological order of discoveries made by some of the researchers who investigated the naked mole-rat.

1840

1842 E. Rüppell publishes a scientific paper, naming the animal *Heterocephalus glaber.*

1950

mid-1950s W. Hill first describes a method of live capture later used by Jarvis and Brett.

mid-1960s J. Jarvis begins her studies of physiology and behavior, establishing colonies in her lab.

1960

1960s B. McNab studies metabolic rate.

1900

early 1900s Scientists from Great Britain and Germany collect specimens in Africa. Debate begins regarding species identification.

1970

mid-1970s K. Johansen and G. Maloiy study respiration and blood hemoglobin.

1976 R. Alexander presents a hypothesis what a eusocial mammal would be like if it existed. Jarvis realizes that the naked mole-rat fits this definition.

1940

1980

1910

1920s W. Hamilton begins to dissect specimens to study anatomy. His work alerts American zoologists to the animal's unique characteristics.

1920

1930

1979 Alexander and P. Sherman bring colonies into their U.S. labs.

1980 Sherman and E. Lacey begin to study division of labor.

Perhaps you'll discover a new eusocial organism where no one has looked. Or you'll learn new information about the social life of an animal that has never been studied before. Many species on earth, especially small ones and those that live where we can't easily see them, remain uninvestigated. By observing and testing hypotheses the way naked mole-rat researchers have, you may solve new mysteries about the world of nature.

Meanwhile, if you'd like to meet a naked mole-rat up close and personal, you can! Zoos in all parts of the world, including the United States, have displays of naked mole-rat colonies where you can watch the animals in action. You may think they're weird looking because you've never seen a naked rodent before. But just remember that maybe we humans look strange too compared to all our hairy relatives, the apes and monkeys.

Visit with the naked mole-rats for a while, and you'll see why biologists think these ugly, little, wrinkly skinned creatures are fascinating, and, in their own way, beautiful!

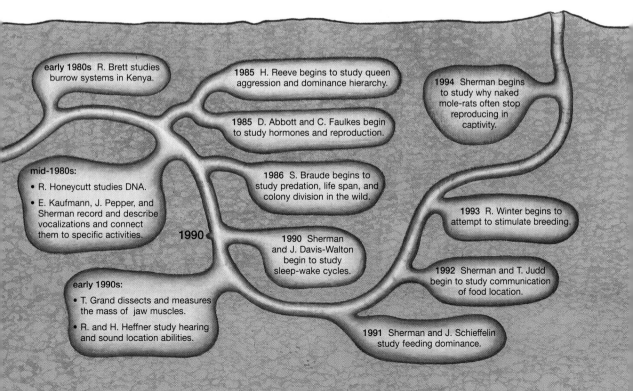

early 1980s R. Brett studies burrow systems in Kenya.

1985 H. Reeve begins to study queen aggression and dominance hierarchy.

1994 Sherman begins to study why naked mole-rats often stop reproducing in captivity.

1985 D. Abbott and C. Faulkes begin to study hormones and reproduction.

mid-1980s:

• R. Honeycutt studies DNA.

• E. Kaufmann, J. Pepper, and Sherman record and describe vocalizations and connect them to specific activities.

1986 S. Braude begins to study predation, life span, and colony division in the wild.

1993 R. Winter begins to attempt to stimulate breeding.

1990

1990 Sherman and J. Davis-Walton begin to study sleep-wake cycles.

1992 Sherman and T. Judd begin to study communication of food location.

early 1990s:

• T. Grand dissects and measures the mass of jaw muscles.

• R. and H. Heffner study hearing and sound location abilities.

1991 Sherman and J. Schieffelin study feeding dominance.

Glossary

cecotrophes—soft, partially digested pellets of feces eaten to replenish protozoa and provide nourishment

cooperatively breeding group—a group in which only a few individuals reproduce, and other members help raise the young

division of labor—a social system in which each individual of the group performs a specific job

DNA (deoxyribonucleic acid)—the chemical substance (molecule) in all organisms that contains the genetic information that is passed from parents to their young

ectothermic—having a body temperature dependent on the environment because the organism's body lacks insulation, so its internal heat is lost to its surroundings

endothermic—having a body temperature independent of an organism's environment that is created by the organism and retained within the organism by insulation

eusocial—truly social; living in a large family group in which only a few members produce all the offspring, and nonbreeding members defend and maintain the colony

gene—a segment of DNA. The basic unit of heredity that determines the characteristics that offspring inherit from their parents.

hemoglobin—the protein that carries oxygen in the blood

homeothermic—having a body temperature that stays the same despite changes in the animal's surrounding environment; commonly called warm-blooded

metabolic rate—the speed of chemical and physical processes within the body. These processes produce energy for the body to use and heat to keep it warm.

physiology—the study of how body processes and parts work

pineal gland—a gland in the brain of animals with backbones, which is believed to control some of the body's responses to light

poikilothermic—having a body temperature that changes when the temperature of the surrounding environment changes; commonly called cold-blooded

reproductive division of labor—a social system in which only a few individuals in a group mate and give birth

vertebrae—the small bones that make up the backbone

Index

Pages listed in **bold** *type refer to photographs.*